READING FOR TODAY
ISSUES 3

FIFTH EDITION

LORRAINE C. SMITH
AND
NANCY NICI MARE

English Language Institute
Queens College
The City University of New York

NATIONAL
GEOGRAPHIC
LEARNING

Australia · Brazil · Mexico · Singapore · United Kingdom · United States

NATIONAL GEOGRAPHIC
LEARNING

Reading for Today 3: Issues
Fifth Edition
Lorraine C. Smith and Nancy Nici Mare

Publisher: Sherrise Roehr

Executive Editor: Laura Le Dréan

Acquisitions Editor: Jennifer Monaghan

Senior Development Editor:
Mary Whittemore

Editorial Assistant: Jennifer Williams-Rapa

Director of Marketing: Ian Martin

Executive Marketing Manager: Ben Rivera

Product Marketing Manager: Dalia Bravo

Senior Director, Production:
Michael Burggren

Content Production Manager:
Mark Rzeszutek

Senior Print Buyer: Mary Beth Hennebury

Compositor: Lumina Datamatics, Inc.

Cover and Interior Design:
Brenda Carmichael

Cover Photo: Looking up at a spiral
staircase, London. Photographer:
Tobias Helbig.

For product information and technology assistance, contact us at
Cengage Learning Customer & Sales Support, cengage.com/contact

For permission to use material from this text or product,
submit all requests online at **cengage.com/permissions**
Further permissions questions can be emailed to
permissionrequest@cengage.com

ISBN-13: 978-1-305-57998-9

National Geographic Learning
20 Channel Center Street
Boston, MA 02210
USA

National Geographic Learning, a Cengage Learning Company, has a mission to bring the world to the classroom and the classroom to life. With our English language programs, students learn about their world by experiencing it. Through our partnerships with National Geographic and TED Talks, they develop the language and skills they need to be successful global citizens and leaders.

Locate your local office at **international.cengage.com/region**

Visit National Geographic Learning online at **NGL.Cengage.com/ELT**
Visit our corporate website at **www.cengage.com**

Printed in the United States of America
Print Number: 04 Print Year: 2020

CONTENTS

SCOPE & SEQUENCE

Unit & Theme	Chapter & Title	Reading Skills	Vocabulary Skills	Critical Thinking Skills
UNIT 1 **The Importance of Time** Page 2	**CHAPTER 1** Our Internal Clock: It's about time Page 4	Using a chart to answer questions Previewing a reading Recalling information Scanning for information Summarizing information **Reading Skill Focus:** Using a Venn diagram	Understanding meaning from context **Word Forms:** Identifying parts of speech: nouns and verbs Understanding synonyms	Creating a survey Comparing results Identifying reasons Evaluating sleep patterns
	CHAPTER 2 Is it OK to be late? Page 18	Previewing a reading Recalling information Scanning for information Summarizing information **Reading Skill Focus:** Creating a flowchart	Understanding meaning from context **Word Forms:** Recognizing the suffix -ing Understanding antonyms	Explaining opinions Comparing cultural differences Discussing adaptation to new places
	CHAPTER 3 Technology competes with family time Page 32	Previewing a reading Recalling information Scanning for information Activating prior knowledge Summarizing information **Reading Skill Focus:** Understanding a Venn diagram	Understanding meaning from context **Word Forms:** Identifying parts of speech: nouns and verbs Understanding words with multiple meanings Choosing the correct dictionary definition	Discussing effects of technology Analyzing changing technology Creating and comparing lists Comparing electronic and personal communication
UNIT 2 **Issues in Today's Society** Page 50	**CHAPTER 4** Sign Language for Everyone Page 52	Previewing a reading Recalling information Scanning for information Summarizing information **Reading Skill Focus:** Using headings to create an outline	Understanding meaning from context **Word Forms:** Understanding word forms: nouns and adjectives Choosing the correct dictionary definition	Describing non-verbal communication Describing reasons Evaluating information Assessing advantages and disadvantages of an operation

SCOPE & SEQUENCE

Unit & Theme	Chapter & Title	Reading Skills	Vocabulary Skills	Critical Thinking Skills
	CHAPTER 5 Our kids are growing up too fast! Page 68	Previewing a reading Scanning for information Recalling information Summarizing information **Reading Skill Focus:** Organizing information in a chart	Understanding meaning from context **Word Forms:** Recognizing the suffix -ment Understanding synonyms	Discussing and comparing reasons Writing about personal experiences Discussing social changes and pressures
	CHAPTER 6 Loneliness: How can we overcome it? Page 82	Previewing a reading Scanning for information Recalling information Summarizing information **Reading Skill Focus:** Creating a flowchart	Understanding meaning from context **Word Forms:** Recognizing the suffix -ness Recognizing sentence connectors	Surveying classmates about loneliness Analyzing survey results Writing about personal experiences Talking about obstacles
UNIT 3 **Justice and Crime** Page 98	**CHAPTER 7** Solving Crimes with Modern Technology Page 100	Previewing a reading Scanning for information Recalling information Summarizing information **Reading Skill Focus:** Understanding line graphs	Understanding meaning from context **Word Forms:** Recognizing the suffix -ment Recognizing the prefix re-	Explaining opinions Creating a list Analyzing information Researching fingerprint matching
	CHAPTER 8 The Reliability of Eyewitnesses Page 116	Previewing a reading Scanning for information Recalling information **Reading Skill Focus:** Using headings to create an outline	Understanding meaning from context **Word Forms:** Recognizing the suffixes -ence and -ance Recognizing the prefix in-	Writing about a crime or an accident Discussing the reliability of eyewitness testimony Organizing importance of details Analyzing information Ranking information

SCOPE & SEQUENCE

Unit & Theme	Chapter & Title	Reading Skills	Vocabulary Skills	Critical Thinking Skills
	CHAPTER 9 Innocent until Proven Guilty: The Criminal Court System Page 132	Previewing a reading Scanning for information Understanding questions Recalling information Summarizing information **Reading Skill Focus:** Creating a flowchart	Understanding meaning from context **Word Forms:** Recognizing the suffix -ity Understanding antonyms	Interpreting symbolism Evaluating a process Applying current events Considering advantages and disadvantages Comparing legal systems
UNIT 4 **Advances in Science** Page 150	**CHAPTER 10** Saving Lives with New Organs Page 152	Previewing a reading Predicting content Scanning for information Recalling information Summarizing information **Reading Skill Focus:** Understanding a bar graph	Understanding meaning from context **Word Forms:** Recognizing the suffixes -tion and -ation Recognizing sentence connectors	Discussing ethics of organ and cell transplants Using graphs Discussing reasons Writing about scenarios
	CHAPTER 11 Objects from Space: Hits and Misses Page 168	Previewing a reading Predicting content Scanning for information Recalling information Summarizing information **Reading Skill Focus:** Understanding graphics	Understanding meaning from context **Word Forms:** Adverbs: recognizing the suffix -ly Recognizing the prefix un-	Presenting research findings Creating a plan of action Describing an experience Evaluating types of natural disasters Discussing reasons
	CHAPTER 12 Medicine Today: Improving Surgery with Robotics Page 184	Previewing a reading Scanning for information Recalling information Summarizing information **Reading Skill Focus:** Understanding a line graph	Understanding meaning from context **Word Forms:** Recognizing the suffix -ment Choosing the correct dictionary definition	Writing about medical technology Considering uses of robots Preparing a report Describing a procedure Creating a list of interview questions

PREFACE

Issues for Today, Fifth Edition, is a reading skills text intended for intermediate, academically-oriented, English-as-a-second or foreign-language (ESL/EFL) students. The topics in this text are fresh and timely, and the book has a strong global focus. As students work with the materials in each chapter, they develop the kinds of extensive and intensive reading skills they will need to achieve academic success in English.

Issues for Today is one in a series of five reading skills texts. The complete series, *Reading for Today,* has been designed to meet the needs of students from the beginning to the advanced levels and includes the following:

- *Reading for Today 1: Themes for Today*   beginning
- *Reading for Today 2: Insights for Today*   high-beginning
- *Reading for Today 3: Issues for Today*   intermediate
- *Reading for Today 4: Concepts for Today*   high-intermediate
- *Reading for Today 5: Topics for Today*   advanced

Issues for Today, Fifth Edition, provides students with essential practice in the types of reading skills they will need in an academic environment. It requires students not only to read text but also to extract basic information from various kinds of charts, graphs, illustrations, and photos. Beginning-level students are rarely exposed to this type of reading material. In addition, they are given the opportunity to speak and write about their own cultures and compare their experiences with those of students from other countries. The text includes real-life activities that give students tasks to complete outside the classroom. These tasks provide students with opportunities to practice reading, writing, speaking, and listening to English in the real world. Thus, all four skills are incorporated into each chapter.

Issues for Today, Fifth Edition, has been designed for flexible use by teachers and students. The text consists of four units. Each unit contains three chapters that deal with related topics. At the same time, though, each chapter is entirely separate in terms of content from the other chapters in that unit. This gives the instructor the option of either completing entire units or choosing individual chapters as the focus in class. Although the chapters are organized by level of difficulty, the teacher and students may choose to work with the chapters out of order, depending on available time and the interests of the class. The activities and exercises in each chapter have been organized to flow from general comprehension—including main ideas and supporting details—through vocabulary in context to critical thinking skills. However, the teacher may choose to work on certain exercises in any order, depending on time and on the students' abilities.

The opening photos and the *Prereading* section before each reading help activate the students' background knowledge of the topic and encourage them to think about the ideas, facts, and vocabulary that will be presented in the reading passage. In fact, discussing photos in class helps lower-level students visualize what they are going to read about and gives them cues for the new vocabulary they will encounter. The exercises that follow the reading passage are intended to develop and improve reading proficiency, including the ability to learn new vocabulary from context and better comprehend English sentence structure. The activities also give students the opportunity to master useful vocabulary encountered in the reading passages through pair work and group discussions that lead them through comprehension of main ideas and specific information.

Intermediate-level language students need considerable visual reinforcement of ideas and vocabulary. Therefore, this text includes many photos and graphics that illustrate the ideas and concepts from the reading passages. In addition, many of the follow-up activities enable students to manipulate the information from the reading passages and other content from the chapter. In fact, the teacher may want the students to complete the charts and lists in the activities on the board.

Vocabulary is recycled throughout each chapter. Experience has shown that low-level students especially need a lot of exposure to the same vocabulary and word forms. Repetition of vocabulary in varied contexts helps students not only understand the new vocabulary better, but also remember it.

A student-centered approach facilitates learning. Wherever possible, students should be actively engaged through pair work or small group work. Except during the actual process of reading, students should be actively engaged in almost all of the activities and exercises with a partner or in a small group. By working with others, students have more opportunities to interact in English. Student group work also allows the teacher to circulate in the classroom and give more individual attention to students than would be possible if the teacher were to direct the class work from the front of the room.

As students work through *Issues for Today*, they will learn and improve their reading skills and develop more confidence in their increasing proficiency in English. At the same time, teachers will be able to observe students' steady progress toward skillful, independent reading.

New to the Fifth Edition

The fifth edition of *Issues for Today* maintains the effective approach of the fourth edition with several significant improvements.

The fifth edition of *Issues for Today* incorporates a number of revisions as well as new material. Four completely new chapters have been added: *Our Internal Clock: It's about Time* in Unit 1, *Our kids are growing up too fast!* in Unit 2, *Saving Lives with New Organs*, and *Objects from Space: Hits and Misses* in Unit 4. All other readings throughout the text have been updated as well. The first exercise in the *Vocabulary Skills* section, *Recognizing Word Forms*, has been revised to put the items in the context of the reading. This makes a clearer connection between the reading passage and the exercise. A second exercise has been added to this section that focuses on various vocabulary skills, such as antonyms, synonyms, and sentence connectors. A new *Reading Skill* section focuses on a specific reading skill, for example, understanding graphs and charts, creating flowcharts, and creating Venn diagrams. Also new to the fifth addition is a *Critical Thinking* section. The activities in this section encourage students to use the information and vocabulary from the reading passages both orally and in writing, and to think beyond the reading passage and form their own opinions. In addition, the fifth edition includes new photos, graphs, and charts, all of which are designed to enhance students' comprehension of the readings. Finally, there is a crossword puzzle at the end of each chapter that reinforces the vocabulary in that particular reading.

These enhancements to *Issues for Today, Fifth Edition,* have been made to help students improve their reading skills, to reinforce vocabulary, and to encourage interest in the topics. These skills are intended to prepare students for academic work and the technical world of information they are about to encounter.

How to Use This Book

Each chapter in this book consists of the following:

- *Prereading*
- *Reading Passage*
- *Fact Finding*
- *Reading Analysis*
- *Vocabulary Skills*
- *Vocabulary in Context*
- *Reading Skill*
- *Information Recall*
- *Topics for Discussion and Writing*
- *Critical Thinking*
- *Crossword Puzzle*

The format of each chapter in the book is consistent. Although each chapter can be done entirely in class, some exercises may be assigned for homework. This, of course, depends on the individual teacher's preference, as well as the availability of class time. Each chapter consists of the following sections:

Prereading

The *Prereading* activity is designed to activate students' background knowledge, stimulate their interest, and provide preliminary vocabulary for the passage itself. The importance of prereading activities should not be underestimated. Studies have shown the positive effect of prereading in motivating students and in enhancing reading comprehension. In fact, prereading discussion in general and discussion of visuals have been shown to be very effective in improving reading comprehension. Students need to spend time describing and discussing the photos and the prereading questions. Furthermore, students should try to relate the topic to their own experience and try to predict what they are going to read about. The teacher can facilitate the students' discussions by writing their guesses and predictions about the reading on the board. This procedure helps motivate students by providing a reason for reading. This process also helps the teacher evaluate the students' knowledge of the content they are about to read in order to provide any necessary background information. After they have read the passage, students can check their predictions for accuracy. The important point to keep in mind is not whether the students' guesses are correct, but rather that they think about the reading beforehand and formulate predictions about the text. Once students have considered the title, the accompanying photos, and the prereading questions, they are ready to read the passage.

Reading Passage

As students read the passage for the first time, they should be encouraged to read for general ideas. After students read the passage to themselves, the teacher may want to read the passage aloud to them. At lower levels, students are very eager to learn pronunciation and feel that this practice is helpful to them. Moreover, reading aloud provides students with an appropriate model for pronunciation and intonation, and helps them hear how words are grouped together by meaning. Students can also listen to the readings on the Audio CD.

Students may wish to maintain individual records of their reading rate. They can keep track of the time it takes them to read a passage for the first time and then record the length of time it takes them to read it a second time. Students should be encouraged to read a text from beginning to end without stopping and to read at a steady pace, reading words in meaningful groups or phrases. Once they have established a base time for reading, they can work to improve their reading rate as they progress through the book.

Fact Finding

After the first reading, students will have a general idea of the information in the passage. The purpose of the *Fact Finding* exercises is to check students' general comprehension. Students will read the *True/False* statements and check whether the information is true or false. If the statement is false, students will go back to the passage and find the line(s) that contain the correct information. They will then rewrite the statement so that it is true. This activity can be done individually or in pairs. Doing this exercise in pairs allows students to discuss their answers with their partner, and to explain their reasons for deciding if a statement is true or false. When all the students have finished the exercise, they can report their answers to the class.

Reading Analysis

At this point, students have read the passage at least three times and should be familiar with the main idea and the content of the reading. The *Reading Analysis* exercise gives students an opportunity to learn new vocabulary from context. In this exercise, students read questions and answer them. This exercise requires students to think about the meanings of words and phrases, the structure of sentences and paragraphs, and the relationships of ideas to each other. This exercise is very effective when done in pairs or in groups. Students can also work individually, but working together provides an excellent opportunity for students to discuss possible answers.

Vocabulary Skills

This section consists of two parts. The first part focuses on recognizing word forms. As an introduction to this exercise, it is recommended that teachers first review parts of speech, especially verbs, nouns, adjectives, and adverbs. Teachers should point out the position of each word form in a sentence. Students will develop a sense for which part of speech is missing in a given sentence. Teachers should also point out clues to verb form and number, and whether an idea is affirmative or negative. Each section has its own instructions, depending on the particular pattern that is being introduced. For example, in the section containing words that take -*tion* in the noun form, teachers can explain that in the exercise students will look at the verb and noun forms of these words. Teachers can use the examples in the directions for each chapter's *Recognizing Word Forms* section to see that the students understand the exercise. All of the sentences in this exercise are content specific, which helps not only reinforce the vocabulary, but also helps check the students' comprehension of the passage. This activity is very effective when done in pairs because students can discuss their answers. After students have a working knowledge of this type of exercise, it can be assigned for homework. The focus of Part 2 of the *Vocabulary Skills* section varies. The purpose of this section is to provide students with a range of ways to learn and practice new vocabulary, and make logical connections by working with words that are commonly paired or that are related to a particular topic. The exercises in this section focus on a variety of important vocabulary-related topics, such as antonyms, synonyms, sentence connectors, prefixes, and dictionary usage.

Vocabulary in Context

This is a fill-in exercise designed as a review of the vocabulary items covered in the *Reading Analysis* and/or *Recognizing Word Forms* exercises. In this exercise, the target words are used in new sentences, giving the students the opportunity to practice the new vocabulary. It can be assigned for homework as a review or done in class as group work.

Reading Skill

Each chapter includes a new *Reading Skill* section which provides instruction and practice with a specific reading skill, such as understanding line or bar graphs, or creating a flowchart, an outline, or a Venn diagram. This section is very effective when done in pairs or small groups. The exercises in these sections may also be done individually, but group work gives the students an opportunity to discuss their work.

Information Recall

This section requires students to review the passage again, in some cases along with the previous Reading Skill exercise, and answer questions that test the students' overall comprehension of the chapter. In addition, students must also write a short summary of the passage using no more than four sentences. In early chapters, the first two sentences are given as a guide.

Topics for Discussion and Writing

This section provides ideas or questions for students to think about and work on alone, in pairs, or in small groups. Students are encouraged to use the information and vocabulary from the passages both orally and in their writing. The writing assignments may be done entirely in class, started in class and finished at home, or done entirely for homework. The last activity in this section is a journal-writing assignment that provides students with an opportunity to reflect on the topic of the chapter and respond to it in some personal way. Students should be encouraged to keep a journal and to write in it regularly. The students' journal writing may be purely personal, or students may choose to have the teacher read their entries. If the teacher reads the entries, the journals should be considered a free-writing activity and should be responded to rather than corrected.

Critical Thinking

This section contains various activities appropriate to the information in the passages. Some activities are designed for pair and small group work. Students are encouraged to use the information and vocabulary from the passages both orally and in writing. The critical thinking questions and activities provide students with an opportunity to think about some aspect of the chapter topic and to share their own thoughts and opinions about it. The goal of this section is for students to go beyond the reading itself and to form their own ideas and opinions on aspects of the topic. Teachers may also use these questions and activities as homework or in-class assignments. The activities in the *Critical Thinking* sections help students interact with the real world as many exercises require students to go outside the classroom to collect specific information.

Crossword Puzzle

The *Crossword Puzzle* in each chapter is based on the vocabulary addressed in that chapter. Students can go over the puzzle orally if pronunciation practice with letters is needed. Teachers can have the students spell out their answers in addition to pronouncing the words themselves. Students invariably enjoy doing crossword puzzles. They are a fun way to reinforce the vocabulary presented in the various exercises in each chapter. Crossword puzzles also require students to pay attention to correct spelling. If the teacher prefers, students can do the *Crossword Puzzle* on their own or with a partner in their free time, or after they have completed an in-class assignment and are waiting for the rest of their classmates to finish.

Index of Key Words and Phrases

The *Index of Key Words and Phrases* is at the back of the book. This section contains words and phrases from all the chapters for easy reference. The *Index of Key Words and Phrases* may be useful to students to help them locate words they need or wish to review.

Skills Index

The *Skills Index* lists the different skills presented and/or practiced in the book.

ACKNOWLEDGMENTS

The authors and publisher would like to thank the following reviewers:

Sola Armanious, Hudson County Community College; **Marina Broeder**, Mission College; **Kara Chambers**, Mission College; **Peter Chin**, Waseda University International; **Feri Collins**, BIR Training Center; **Courtney DeRouen**, University of Washington; **Jeanne de Simon**, University of West Florida; **Shoshana Dworkin**, BIR Training Center; **Cindy Etter**, University of Washington International and English Language Programs; **Ken Fackler**, University of Tennessee at Martin; **Jan Hinson**, Carson Newman University; **Chigusa Katoku**, Mission College; **Sharon Kruzic**, Mission College; **Carmella Lieskle**, Shimane University; **Yelena Malchenko**, BIR Training Center; **Mercedes Mont**, Miami Dade College; **Ewa Paluch**, BIR Training Center; **Barbara Pijan**, Portland State University, Intensive English Language Program; **Julaine Rosner**, Mission College; **Julie Scales**, University of Washington; **Mike Sfiropoulos**, Palm Beach State College; **Barbara Smith-Palinkas**, Hillsborough Community College; **Eileen Sotak**, BIR Training Center; **Matthew Watterson**, Hongik University; **Tristinn Williams**, IELP—University of Washington; **Iryna Zhylina**, Hudson County Community College; **Ana Zuljevic**, BIR Training Center

Acknowledgments from Authors
We are thankful to everyone at Cengage, especially Laura Le Dréan, Mary Whittemore, Jennifer Monaghan, Patricia Giunta, and Yeny Kim for their unwavering support. We are extremely grateful to all the teachers and students who use our book and who never hesitate to give us such incredible feedback. As always, we are very appreciative of the ongoing encouragement from our families, friends, and colleagues.

.

L.C.S. and N.N.M.

Dedication:
To Joseph

The Importance
of Time

1. Are you a very busy person? Do you have a lot of free time every day?

2. Do you have enough time to do everything you need to do?

3. Do you look at your watch or cell phone a lot to see the time? Why or why not?

Waiting for a subway, France

CHAPTER **1** Our Internal Clock: It's about time

Prereading

1. What time do you do the activities in the chart below? Write your answers in the chart. Then ask three classmates about each activity. Write their names and answers in the chart.

What time do you do these activities?			
Activity	You	Name: _____	Name: _____	Name: _____
wake up				
eat breakfast				
eat lunch				
eat dinner				
go to bed				

2. What similarities do you see between your schedule and your classmates' schedules? How are they similar? How are they different?

3. Do you sometimes eat before you go to bed? Do you think this is a good idea? Why or why not?

4. Read the title of this article. What do you think this article is about?

Reading

Read the passage carefully. Then complete the exercises that follow.

Our Internal Clock: It's about time

1   Many people enjoy a late-night snack before bedtime. It's not uncommon to
2   have a little something to eat before going to bed—perhaps a sandwich or a bowl
3   of ice cream. It's not unusual, but it may be unhealthy. Many medical reports have
4   already shown that late-night eating often makes people gain weight. Furthermore,
5   new scientific studies show that frequent late-night eating can also affect learning
6   and memory.
7   All humans have an "internal clock." This internal clock influences when we sleep,
8   wake up, and feel hungry. Our internal clocks have a 24-hour cycle that tells us when
9   to go to bed. Eating at the wrong time of the day upsets this cycle. Eating when we
10 should be sleeping is even worse. This is because our body needs to sleep at a certain
11 time. When we eat late, we often go to sleep even later, which disrupts, or changes,
12 our internal clocks even more.
13   Christopher Colwell is a professor of psychiatry at the UCLA School of Medicine
14 in California in the United States. For years he has studied the cycle of sleeping and
15 waking up. He believes that this cycle impacts learning and memory. "Disrupting
16 that sleep-wake cycle is bad for our health," says Colwell. He believes it can affect
17 our brain and how we learn and remember information.
18   Professor Colwell studied two groups of mice as part of his research. In the
19 experiment, the researchers fed one group of mice at their regular time. The
20 researchers fed the second group of mice during their normal sleep time. All of the
21 mice ate the same amount of food and slept the same number of hours. There was

22 only one difference: The second group of mice ate and went to sleep at a time that was
23 different from their usual schedule. After a few weeks, the researchers gave learning
24 tests to all the mice. The mice that ate during their regular sleep time had problems
25 with memory. It was difficult for them to remember what they already learned.
26 Colwell also saw changes in their hippocampus. The hippocampus is the part of the
27 brain used for learning and memory. Although Colwell used mice in this experiment,
28 he believes this result is true for people, too.
29   Colwell's conclusions were clear. "Having a strong sleep-wake cycle is good for
30 our health. That means eating at the right times," says Colwell. "If we're going on
31 vacation, it's no big deal." Vacations are usually short and do not have any lasting
32 effects. However, if we frequently eat when we should be asleep, we are disrupting
33 our internal clock. As a result, we may experience learning and memory problems.
34 It's important to pay attention to our internal clock!

A mouse taking a memory test, Princeton University, Princeton, New Jersey

Fact Finding

Read the passage again. Then read the following statements. Check (√) whether each statement is True or False. If a statement is false, rewrite it so that it is true. Then go back to the passage and find the line that supports your answer.

1. _____ True _____ False   Eating late at night may be unhealthy.

_____

2. _____ True _____ False   Our internal clock tells us when to go to school.

_____

3. _____ True _____ False   Professor Colwell studies the importance of the sleep-wake cycle.

_____

4. _____ True _____ False   All of the mice in the study ate at the same time.

_____

5. _____ True _____ False   Some of the mice in the experiment slept more hours than other mice.

_____

6. _____ True _____ False   Professor Colwell saw changes in the brains of all the mice in the experiment.

_____

7. _____ True _____ False   Professor Colwell believes that eating and sleeping at the same time every day helps learning and memory.

_____

Reading Analysis

Read each question carefully. Circle the letter or the number of the correct answer.

1. Read lines 1–6.

    a. A late-night snack before bedtime means

       1. you eat a big meal before you go to bed.

       2. you eat a little food before you go to sleep.

       3. you eat some food in your bed.

b. Which word is a synonym for **uncommon**?
   1. Unusual
   2. Unhealthy
   3. Frequent

c. In line 2, what follows the dash (—)?
   1. A definition
   2. Additional information
   3. An example

d. When people **gain** weight, they
   1. become heavier.
   2. become thinner.
   3. become healthier.

e. In line 4, what does **furthermore** mean?
   1. In addition
   2. However
   3. As a result

2. Read lines 7–10.
   a. What is our **"internal clock"**?
      1. Something inside our bodies that tells us when to eat and sleep
      2. An alarm clock near our beds that wakes us up
      3. Something that helps us to learn and remember

   b. **Influences** means
      1. changes.
      2. causes.
      3. teaches.

   c. What is a **24-hour cycle**?
      1. Several activities that repeat every day at the same time
      2. 24 activities that go around in a circle
      3. A complete day of 24 hours

   d. These sentences mean that **eating when we should be sleeping is even worse** than
      1. eating a bowl of ice cream or a sandwich.
      2. sleeping when we should be eating.
      3. eating at the wrong time during the day.

3. Read lines 10–12.
   a. **A certain time** means
      1. a different time every day.
      2. a particular time every day.
      3. a new time every day.

    b. **Disrupts** means

       1. studies.

       2. changes.

       3. understands.

    c. What is a synonym for **disrupts**?

       1. Upsets

       2. Helps

       3. Needs

4. Read lines 15–16. Which word is a synonym for **impacts**?

    a. Cycles

    b. Disturbs

    c. Affects

5. Read lines 16–18. **He believes it can affect our brain....**
The pronoun **it** refers to

    a. learning and memory.

    b. studying psychiatry.

    c. disrupting our sleep-wake cycle.

6. Read paragraph 4. What was the difference between the two groups of mice?

    a. They ate different amounts of food.

    b. They went to sleep at different times.

    c. They slept a different number of hours.

7. Read lines 19–21. What word is a synonym for **normal**?

    a. Different

    b. Same

    c. Regular

8. In line 26, what is the **hippocampus**?

    a. A part of the brain

    b. An internal clock

    c. The sleep-wake cycle

9. In line 29, **conclusions** means

    a. opinions.

    b. results.

    c. cycles.

10. Read lines 30–32.

    a. **It's no big deal** means

       1. it's not important.

       2. it's not necessary.

       3. it's not good.

b. **"If we're going on vacation, it's no big deal"** means

   1. it's a very good idea to take a vacation.
   2. it's OK to change your sleep-wake cycle for a short time.
   3. you can never change your sleep-wake cycle.

11. Read lines 31–32. **Lasting** means

   a. continuing.
   b. ending.
   c. growing.

12. What is the main idea of the passage?

   a. We all have internal clocks that influence when we eat, sleep, and wake up.
   b. In the experiment, the mice that ate during their regular sleep time had memory problems.
   c. Eating when you should be sleeping can have a bad effect on learning and memory.

Vocabulary Skills

PART 1

Recognizing Word Forms
In English, the verb and noun forms of some words are the same, for example, *study (v.), study (n.)*.

Complete each sentence with the correct form of the word on the left. Then circle *(v.)* if you are using a verb or *(n.)* if you are using a noun. Write all the verbs in the simple present. The nouns may be singular or plural.

cause **1.** Professor Colwell believes that eating late at night _____ health
               (v.) / (n.)

   problems. He studies the _____ of some changes in the brains of mice.
                            (v.) / (n.)

impact **2.** Our internal clocks have a big _____ on learning and memory. Late-night
                  (v.) / (n.)

   eating greatly _____ sleep-wake cycles.
                  (v.) / (n.)

report   **3.** Many medical _____ show that people gain weight when they eat right
                        (v.) / (n.)

before they go to bed. Doctors often _____ this information to their patients.
                                              (v.) / (n.)

snack   **4.** Some people never _____ late at night. They only eat a few
                        (v.) / (n.)

_____ early in the day.
    (v.) / (n.)

study   **5.** Professor Colwell _____ the sleep-wake cycle in mice. It's a very important
                        (v.) / (n.)

_____.
    (v.) / (n.)

PART 2

Synonyms

Synonyms are words with similar meanings. For example, *sad* and *unhappy* are synonyms.

Match each word or phrase with its synonym. Write the letter of the correct answer and the word or phrase in the space provided.

c. influence   1. affect   a. continuing

_____ 2. certain   b. in addition

_____ 3. conclusion   c. ~~influence~~

_____ 4. disrupt   d. inside

_____ 5. furthermore   e. particular

_____ 6. internal   f. result

_____ 7. lasting   g. upset

_____ 8. normal   h. usual

Vocabulary in Context

Read the following sentences. Complete each sentence with the correct word from the box. Use each word only once.

certain *(adj.)*	effects *(n.)*	influences *(v.)*	normal *(adj.)*
cycle *(n.)*	experiments *(n.)*	memory *(n.)*	uncommon *(adj.)*
disturb *(v.)*	furthermore *(adv.)*		

1. My classmates and I often do _____ in our chemistry class.

2. Julie has a very good _____ for new vocabulary. She remembers new words very well.

3. Cars are very _____ in my town. Most people ride bicycles instead.

4. It is _____ to feel tired on Monday mornings after a very busy weekend.

5. Please don't _____ me. I'm trying to study for an important test and I need to concentrate.

6. I always buy a _____ kind of pet food for my dog. He won't eat any other kind!

7. The weather _____ how I go to school. If it's warm, I walk, but if it's cold, I take the bus.

8. Carlos is always very busy. He takes classes at the university five days a week. _____, he works every night and on the weekends.

9. A good diet and exercise have positive _____ on your health.

10. My sleep-wake _____ is very consistent. I always go to sleep and wake up at the same times every day.

Reading Skill

Using a Venn Diagram
Venn diagrams show the differences and similarities between two topics. Using a Venn diagram can help you organize and understand important information from a reading passage.

1. **Read the passage again, and then read the phrases below. Write the phrases in the correct place in the Venn diagram.**

- ate the same amount of food
- ~~slept at a time that was different from their usual sleep time~~
- slept at their regular times
- slept the same number of hours
- ate during their normal sleep time
- ate at their regular times
- had problems with memory

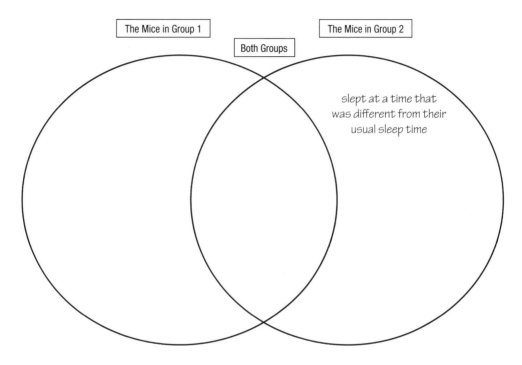

The Mice in Group 1

The Mice in Group 2

Both Groups

slept at a time that was different from their usual sleep time

2. **Read the sentences below. Put a check (√) next to the sentences that are true.**

a. _____ The mice in Groups 1 and 2 ate different amounts of food.

b. _____ The mice in Group 1 ate and slept at their normal times.

c. _____ The mice in Group 2 did not sleep at their normal time.

d. _____ There was no difference in the amount of time that the mice in Groups 1 and 2 slept.

e. _____ The mice in Group 2 ate at their usual time.

f. _____ The mice in Groups 1 and 2 slept the same number of hours.

g. _____ The mice in Group 2 had problems with memory.

Information Recall

Read the passage again, and review the Venn diagram. Then answer the questions.

1. What are two reasons that late-night eating is not a good idea?

   _____

   _____

2. How can we keep our internal clock strong?

   _____

   _____

3. What did Professor Colwell learn from his study with two groups of mice?

   _____

   _____

Writing a Summary

A summary is a short paragraph that provides the most important information from a reading. It usually does not include details, just the main ideas. When you write a summary, it is important to use your own words, and not copy directly from the reading.

Write a brief summary of the passage. It should not be more than four sentences. Use your own words. The first two sentences of the summary are below. Write two more sentences to complete the summary.

Although many people like to eat something late at night, research shows that this habit can be bad for us. We have an internal clock that tells us the best times to eat and sleep so we can stay healthy.

_____

_____

_____

_____

Topics for Discussion and Writing

1. Think about a time when you did not get a good night's sleep. How did you feel the next day? Talk about this with your classmates.

2. Take a survey in class, and ask your classmates these questions: How many hours do you usually sleep every night? Do you think you need more sleep? Why or why not? Then look at the answers from your survey at the beginning of the chapter. Do most of your classmates get enough sleep?

3. Discuss this question with a partner: What are the most common reasons why many college students go to bed very late?

4. Write in your journal. Do you think you have a good sleep-wake cycle? Is it always the same? Why or why not? Explain your reason and give examples.

Critical Thinking

1. Many doctors believe that people gain weight when they eat late at night. What do you think are some reasons for this? Discuss this with a partner, and compare your ideas with your classmates' ideas.

2. Professor Colwell said, "Having a strong sleep-wake cycle is good for our health. That means eating at the right times." How can busy students, who often stay up late studying and eating late-night snacks, change their habits to have a better sleep-wake cycle? What suggestions can you give them?

Crossword Puzzle

Review the words in the box below. Then read the clues on the next page. Write the words in the correct spaces in the puzzle.

affect	experiment	hippocampus	normal
certain	frequent	internal	research
conclusion	furthermore	lasting	snack
cycle	gain	memory	uncommon
disrupt			

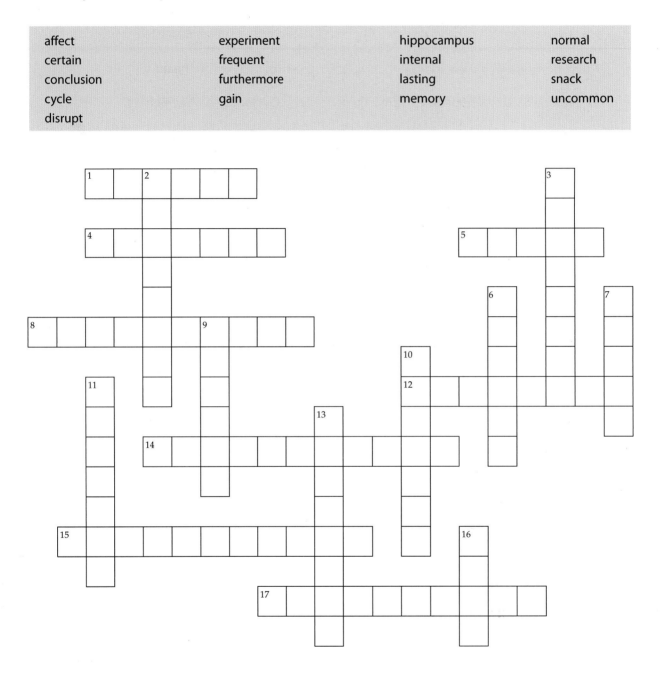

Crossword Puzzle Clues

ACROSS CLUES

1. We should eat and sleep during our _____ eating and sleeping times.

4. Good sleep-wake habits can have a _____ positive effect on our health.

5. When I am hungry, I sometimes have a quick _____, such as a piece of fruit.

8. When scientists study something, they do an _____.

12. Anything inside us is _____.

14. In addition

15. A part of the brain

17. Result

DOWN CLUES

2. Scientific _____ on healthy behavior is very important to us.

3. Unusual

6. Influence

7. Series of repeating activities

9. When we can remember things well, it means we have a good _____.

10. Upset

11. Particular

13. Something that happens often is a _____ event.

16. If we eat too much, we may _____ weight.

Prereading

1. Read each type of appointment or event. What time would you arrive for each one? Write the time for each appointment in the chart. Then compare your responses as a class. What similarities and differences are there in your times of arrival? How might you explain these differences?

Type of Appointment	Scheduled Time	Time You Would Arrive
dentist	9:00 a.m.	8:45
university class	11:00 a.m.	9:45
lunch with a friend at school	12:00 p.m.	12:00
job interview at a bank	2:00 p.m.	1:50
dinner with your spouse	7:00 p.m.	7:00
a friend's party	9:00 p.m.	8:50

2. What does **on time** mean?

not late, on the exact scheduled.

3. Are you usually on time, or are you usually late? Why? _on time. Because it is important to be on time._

4. Is it always important to be on time? Look at the chart on page 18. How important is it to be on time for each appointment or event? Put a check (√) in the box to show your answer. Discuss your answers with the class.

How important is it to be on time?				
Type of Appointment	Scheduled Time	Very Important	A Little Important	Not Important
dentist	9:00 a.m.	✓		
university class	11:00 a.m.	✓		
lunch with a friend at school	12:00 p.m.		✓	
job interview at a bank	2:00 p.m.	✓		
dinner with your spouse	7:00 p.m.	✓		
a friend's party	9:00 p.m.		✓	

5. Read the title of the article. What do you think this passage is about?

Reading

🎧 **Read the passage carefully. Then complete the exercises that follow.**
CD 1
TR 3

Is it OK to be late?

1   In the United States, it is important to be on time, or punctual, for an appointment, a
2   class, a meeting, etc. For an American, being on time means arriving at the exact hour
3   of the scheduled meeting. However, this may not be true in all countries. An American
4   professor discovered this difference while teaching a class at a Brazilian university. The
5   two-hour class was scheduled to begin at 10:00 a.m. and end at 12:00 p.m. On the first
6   day, the professor arrived at 10:00 a.m., which was on time for him as an American. To his
7   surprise, no one was in the classroom. Many students came after 10:00 a.m. Several arrived
8   after 10:30 a.m. Two students came after 11:00 a.m. Although all the students were friendly
9   and greeted the professor as they arrived, few apologized for their lateness. Were these
10   students being rude? Before deciding that they were simply impolite, the professor decided
11   to study the students' behavior.

The professor talked to American and Brazilian students about lateness in both an informal and a formal situation: lunch with a friend and in a university class, respectively. He gave them an example, asked them how they would react, and recorded their answers. If they had a lunch appointment with a friend, the average American student defined lateness as 19 minutes after the agreed time. On the other hand, the average Brazilian student felt the friend was late after 33 minutes.

In an American university, students are expected to arrive at the appointed hour. In contrast, in Brazil, neither the teacher nor the students always arrive at the appointed hour. Classes not only begin at the scheduled time in the United States, but they also end at the scheduled time. In the Brazilian class, only a few students left the class at noon; many remained past 12:30 p.m. to discuss the class and ask more questions. While arriving late may not be very important in Brazil, neither is staying late.

The explanation for these differences is complicated. People from Brazilian and North American cultures have different feelings about lateness. In Brazil, the students believe that a person who usually arrives late is probably more successful than a person who is always on time. In fact, Brazilians expect a person with status or prestige to arrive late, while in the United States lateness is usually considered to be disrespectful and unacceptable. Consequently, if a Brazilian is late for an appointment with a North American, the American may misinterpret the reason for the lateness and become angry.

As a result of his study, the American professor learned that the Brazilian students were not being disrespectful to him. Instead, they were simply behaving in the appropriate way for a Brazilian student in Brazil. Eventually, the professor was able to adapt his own behavior so that he could feel comfortable in the new culture.

Fact Finding

Read the passage again. Then read the following statements. Check (√) whether each statement is True or False. If a statement is false, rewrite it so that it is true. Then go back to the passage and find the line that supports your answer.

1. ____ True _√_ False   On the first day of class, the professor ~~arrived late~~, but the students were on time.
   one time ... *late*

   _____ line 5-7 _____

2. _√_ True ____ False   The professor decided to study the behavior of Brazilian and American students.

   _____

3. _√_ True ____ False   In an American university, it is important to be on time.

   _____

4. ____ True _√_ False   In a Brazilian class, the students leave immediately after the class is finished.

   _____ 21-22 _____

5. _√_ True ____ False   In an American university, many students probably leave immediately after the class is finished.

   _____

6. _√_ True ____ False   Most North Americans think a person who is late is disrespectful.

   _____

7. ____ True _√_ False   In Brazil, most successful people are expected to be on time.

   _____ 25-27 _____

8. ____ True _√_ False   As a result of the study, the professor changed ~~the Brazilian~~ students' behavior.
   his own

   _____ 34-35 _____

Few قلة

Reading Analysis

Read each question carefully. Circle the letter or the number of the correct answer, or write the answer in the space provided.

1. Why did the professor study the Brazilian students' behavior?
   a. The students seemed very rude to him.
   b. He wanted to understand why the students came late.
   c. He wanted to make the students come to class on time.

2. Read lines 1–3.
   a. **Punctual** means
      on time.
   b. How do you know?
   _____

   c. An **appointment** is
      1. a university class.
      2. a punctual time.
      3. a scheduled time for something.

3. Read lines 8–11.
   a. **Greeted** means
      1. said hello.
      2. arrived.
      3. were friendly.
   b. **As** means
      1. because.
      2. when.
      3. if.
   c. What does **few** refer to?
      1. The professor
      2. Students
      3. Greetings
   d. Students **apologized** means
      1. they said they were sorry.
      2. they said hello.
      3. they said they were late.
   e. **Rude** means
      1. impolite.
      2. noisy.
      3. punctual.

f. **Behavior** means
   1. arrival.
   2. speech.
   3. actions.

4. Read lines 12–15.
   a. What is an example of an **informal** situation?

   lunch with a friend

   b. **Informal** means
      1. serious.
      2. casual. _relax_
      3. local.

   c. What is an example of a **formal** situation?

   university class

   d. **Respectively** means
      1. in that order.
      2. usually.
      3. with respect.

   e. **Respectively** helps you understand
      1. what situation was first.
      2. what situation was second.
      3. both 1 and 2.

5. Read lines 14–17.
   a. **React** means
      1. respond.
      2. talk.
      3. arrive.

   b. An **average** American student's answer to the professor's question is
      1. how all the American students answered.
      2. how most of the American students answered.
      3. how a few of the American students answered.

   c. How does **on the other hand** connect the American idea of lateness with the Brazilian idea of lateness?
      1. It shows a similarity.
      2. It gives more information.
      3. It shows a contrast.

6. Read lines 19–20: **Neither the teacher nor the students always arrive at the appointed hour.** Who arrives at the appointed hour?
   a. No one
   b. Only the students
   c. The teacher and the students

7. Read lines 20–21: **Classes not only begin at the scheduled time in the United States, but they also end at the scheduled time.** What does **not only . . . but . . . also** mean?

    a. And

    b. But

    c. So

8. Read lines 25–31.

    a. What does **in fact** indicate?

        1. A contrast between two ideas

        2. Something that is true

        3. Emphasis of the previous idea

    b. A synonym for **status** is

        1. prestige.

        2. disrespect.

        3. anger.

    c. **Disrespectful** means

        1. angry.

        2. unacceptable.

        3. not polite.

    d. **Misinterpret** means

        1. translate.

        2. not understand.

        3. become angry.

9. Read lines 33–35.

    a. What does **instead** show?

        1. A similarity

        2. A substitution

        3. An opposite

    b. **Adapt** means

        1. change to a new situation.

        2. improve a situation.

        3. act a certain way.

10. What is the main idea of the passage?

    a. It is important to be on time for class in the United States.

    b. People learn the importance of time when they are children.

    c. The importance of being on time differs among cultures.

Vocabulary Skills

PART 1

Recognizing Word Forms

In English, there are several ways that verbs change to nouns. Some verbs become nouns by adding the suffix -ing, for example, spell (v.), spelling (n.).

Complete each sentence with the correct word form on the left. Use the correct form of the verb in either the affirmative or the negative form. The nouns may be singular or plural.

feel *(v.)*

feeling *(n.)*

1. Many cultures have different _feelings_ about lateness. In the United States, some people _feel_ that a late person is rude.

understand *(v.)*

understanding *(n.)*

2. At the beginning of the year, the professor _didn't understand_ why the students came late to his class. After he talked to them, his _understanding_ of their behavior improved.

end *(v.)*

ending *(n.)*

3. In the United States, university classes begin and _end verb_ at the scheduled time. The _ending_ of classes usually means the students leave right away.

greet *(v.)*

greeting *(n.)*

4. "Hi," "Hello," and "How are you" are common _greetings_ in the United States. Most people also _greet_ each other with a smile.

meet *(v.)*

meeting *(n.)*

5. Some teachers _meet_ with their students after class to give them extra help. These _meetings_ are very helpful.

PART 2

Antonyms

Antonyms are words that have opposite meanings. For example, *easy* and *difficult* are antonyms.

Match each word with its antonym. Write the letter of the correct answer and the word in the space provided.

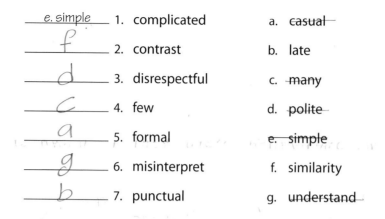

e. simple 1. complicated   a. ~~casual~~

_f_ 2. contrast   b. late

_d_ 3. disrespectful   c. ~~many~~

_c_ 4. few   d. ~~polite~~

_a_ 5. formal   e. ~~simple~~

_g_ 6. misinterpret   f. similarity

_b_ 7. punctual   g. ~~understand~~

Vocabulary in Context

Read the following sentences. Complete each sentence with the correct word or phrase from the box. Use each word or phrase only once.

adapt (v.)	behavior (n.)	~~in fact~~	misinterpreted (v.)	~~punctual (adj.)~~
~~apologized (v.)~~	greets (v.)	~~instead (adv.)~~	prestige (n.)	~~rude (adj.)~~

1. It's too cold today to go to the zoo. Let's go to the museum _instead_.

2. Diane _misinterpreted_ the text message from her brother. He wanted to see her at 9:00 p.m., but she went in the morning and he wasn't home.

3. In most countries, doctors have considerable _prestige_. People respect them very much.

4. Greg always _greets_ people by smiling and saying hello.

5. It was very _rude_ of Martin to ask Ms. Barnes her age.

6. Being _punctual_ for a job interview is important in order to make a good impression.

7. When you walk into a dark room from the bright sunlight, your eyes need a few moments to _adapt_ to the change.

8. It is very cold in Antarctica. _in fact_, it is the coldest place on Earth.

9. Martha dropped chocolate ice cream on my white rug. She _apologized_, but I told her not to worry about it, and we cleaned it up.

10. I don't understand Mark's _behavior_. He gets angry for no reason and refuses to talk to anyone.

Reading Skill

Creating a Flowchart

Flowcharts show certain kinds of information, such as how people study events and how they come to conclusions. Creating a flowchart can help you organize and understand important information from a reading passage.

Reread pages 19–20. Then complete the flowchart with information from the passage.

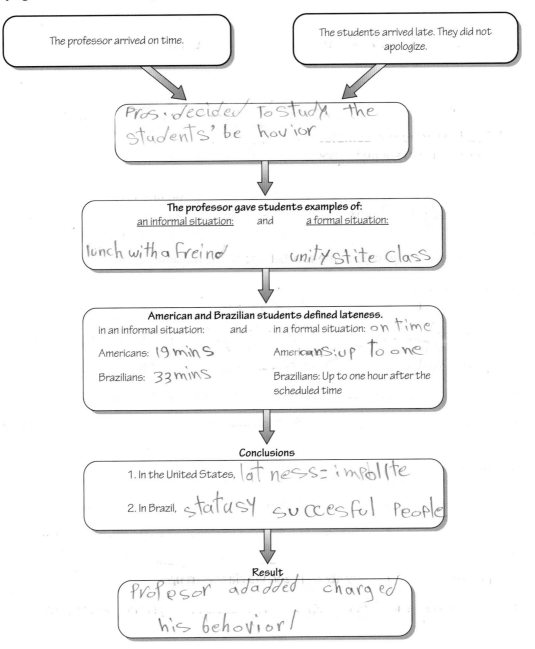

The professor arrived on time.

The students arrived late. They did not apologize.

Pros. decided To Study the students' be hovior

The professor gave students examples of:
an informal situation: and   a formal situation:

lunch with a freind   unity stite class

American and Brazilian students defined lateness.

in an informal situation: and   in a formal situation: on time

Americans: 19 mins   Americans: up to one

Brazilians: 33 mins   Brazilians: Up to one hour after the scheduled time

Conclusions

1. In the United States, lat ness= impolite

2. In Brazil, statusy succesful People

Result

Profesor adadded charged his behovior!

Information Recall

Read the passage again, and review the flowchart. Then answer the questions.

1. Why did the professor decide to study Brazilian and American university students' attitudes about lateness?

   a. _To understend the differences in behover._

   b. _To know if they were being rude or not._

2. What differences did the professor discover between these two groups of students?

   a. _late = impolit (informal -19 mint/formel = ontime)._

   b. _status (_

3. What did the professor do as a result of his study?

   The professor was able to adapt his own behavior so that he could feel comfortable in the new culture

Writing a Summary

A summary is a short paragraph that provides the most important information from a reading. It usually does not include details, just the main ideas. When you write a summary, it is important to use your own words, and not copy directly from the reading.

Write a brief summary of the passage. It should not be more than four sentences. Use your own words. The first sentence of the summary is below. Write three more sentences to complete the summary.

> An American professor teaching in Brazil wondered why his students came to class late, so he decided to study the differences between American and Brazilian students in different situations. _He started to explain and show the differences between both the Americans and Brazillians. Due to his study, both were acting the way they were taught to do in their own culture._

Topics for Discussion and Writing

who is the person late is very rude

1. Describe how people in your culture feel about someone who is late. For example, do you think that person is rude and irresponsible, or do you think that person is prestigious and successful? Explain your answer, and give some examples. *In my culture, being late is disrespectful people would not like and accept that at all, they will think that*

2. When you travel to a new place, what kinds of adaptations or changes (for example, eating different kinds of food, using a different currency, etc.) do you have to make? Explain your answer. *When I travel to a new place, I would have to use a different currency*

3. Write in your journal. Do you think it is important to adapt your behavior to a new culture? What behaviors would you be willing to change? What behaviors would you not be willing to change? Explain. *I think it is very important to adapt my behavior because it is very respectful to act like other new cultures, I will not be willing to change my behavior but I will change because not all countries uses pounds*

Critical Thinking

1. There are many differences in customs among cultures. In the table below, list some cultural differences between this country and your country, or between your country and another country you have visited. Compare your list with your classmates' lists. *other things like food.*

Cultural Difference	Your Country: S	Another Country:
Clothes: school / work	must wear a uniform everyday	most schools do not wear uniforms
food	must take your own food.	students would get food in school
electronics	no electronics allowed	can use laptops and phones.
iterrupting	not allowed to interrupt during class	can interrupt at any time.
heating and cooling	no ac or heat.	ac and heat during school hours.

2. What is the biggest change in your behavior that you need to make when you go to a different country? Do you think this is an easy change? Why or why not? Give reasons and examples. Discuss your ideas with your classmates. *The biggest chang is food because not everyone is willing to change their food routine.*

3. Discuss these questions with a partner: How do you think the professor adapted his behavior in Brazil after his study? Why do you think the professor changed his behavior? Why didn't he try to change the Brazilian students' behavior? *because he did not want them to feel uncomfortable during class.*

Crossword Puzzle

Review the words in the box below. Then read the clues on the next page. Write the words in the correct spaces in the puzzle.

adapt behavior greet punctual
apologize disrespectful informal react
appointment few instead respectively
as format misinterpret status
average

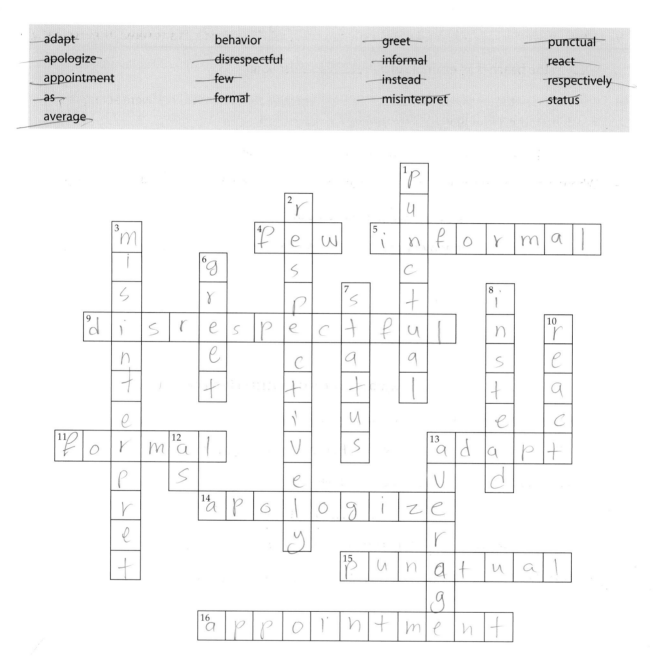

Crossword Puzzle Clues

ACROSS CLUES

4. Although the teacher asked several questions, very ___few___ students answered. They were shy.

5. A day at the beach is an example of a(n) __informal__ situation.

9. The Brazilian students were not __disrespectful__ to the American professor. They were acting appropriately according to their own culture.

11. A wedding is a very __formal__ situation. You can't wear jeans!

13. Whenever we are in a new culture, we need to __adapt__ to different ways of doing things.

14. I __apologize__ for hurting your feelings. I didn't mean it.

15. The professor did an experiment so he could understand the Brazilian students' __punctual__, or actions.

16. I have a(n) __appointment__ with my teacher at 3:00 p.m. today.

DOWN CLUES

1. Being on time, or __punctual__, for a job interview is important in many cultures.

2. Juan and Carla want coffee and tea, __respectively__.

3. Sometimes people __misinterpret__ what I say. However, you always understand me.

6. In most cultures, people __greet__ each other when they meet.

7. A university professor usually has __status__, or prestige.

8. I don't want to study now. I want to study over the weekend __instead__.

10. How did the professor __react__ when the Brazilian students arrived late?

12. The students said good-bye __as__ they left the room.

13. The __average__ of 8, 13, and 15 is 12.

Prereading

1. Look at the photo. Describe it. Who are these people? What are they doing?

2. Answer the questions in the chart below. Then compare your answers with your classmates' answers.

Each week, how much time do you spend	Number of Hours
1. watching TV?	
2. surfing the Internet?	
3. talking on your cell phone?	
4. playing computer games?	
Total Number of Hours 1–4	
5. speaking with your family?	
Difference between 1–4 and 5	

3. Read the title of this chapter, and review your chart.

   a. Do you spend more time using technology or more time with your family?

   b. Is it important to spend time with your family? Why or why not?

Reading

🎧 **Read the passage carefully. Then complete the exercises that follow.**

CD 1
TR 4

Technology competes with family time

1 When the Johnson family bought their first computer several years ago, Mr. and
2 Mrs. Johnson were thrilled that their children had access to so much information
3 through the Internet. Now, though, they're not as excited anymore. "Our family spends
4 more time surfing the Internet than communicating with each other," complains
5 Mr. Johnson. The Johnson family is not alone in this situation. According to research by
6 the Annenberg Center for the Digital Future at the University of Southern California,
7 in 2006, 11 percent of Americans said they were spending less time with their families.
8 Last year, that number almost tripled to 28 percent.
9 It seems that as Internet use becomes more popular, the amount of family time
10 decreases. In other words, when technology competes with family time, technology
11 wins. Many parents are concerned about this reduction in the time their families
12 spend together, and Michael Gilbert agrees. He is a researcher at the Annenberg
13 Center. "Most people think of the Internet and our digital future as boundless—
14 unlimited— and I do, too," Gilbert said. However, he added, "It can't be a good
15 thing that families are spending less face-to-face time together."
16 As technology becomes more advanced, it often changes the ways that families
17 interact. This is not a new concern. When televisions first became popular in the
18 1950s, parents worried that their children were watching too much TV and spending
19 too little time talking with their parents. However, there is a significant difference
20 between these two activities. Watching TV can be done as a family, while surfing the
21 Internet is often a solitary activity. Furthermore, the Internet isn't the only modern
22 technology pushing families apart. Many children today have cell phones. Although
23 they can help parents to keep track of their children, cell phones also give children
24 more privacy. Sometimes they have too much privacy. "When I was a teenager,"
25 Mrs. Johnson says, "my friends telephoned me at home. My parents always knew
26 who was calling me."

Although reduced family time seems to be a pattern for all households, it may be even greater for families with higher incomes. Gilbert reported that 35 percent of higher-income families felt there was a drop in face-to-face time. In addition to reduced face-to-face time among all family members, women say that they feel ignored by a family Internet user. In fact, almost half say they sometimes or often feel ignored when a family member is using the Internet, while fewer than 40 percent of men feel this way.

Gilbert said, "People report spending less time with family members as social networks such as Facebook, Twitter, and Instagram are booming." However, not all young people enjoy the new technology that allows them to be in contact with their friends around the clock. Steven Cho, a college student, is one of them. Every summer he works at a camp in upstate New York. The camp has very little Internet access. "It's nice to get away from the Internet for a few weeks every summer," says Steven. "I can relax and do other things like play music, read, or be with my friends." Although he spends a lot of time on the Internet during the school year, he is happy to have a break from it. "It gets very tiring sometimes," he adds. The Internet is here to stay, and so are cell phones. How will families change in the future as technology competes with their time together?

Fact Finding

Read the passage again. Then read the following statements. Check (√) whether each statement is True or False. If a statement is false, rewrite it so that it is true. Then go back to the passage and find the line that supports your answer.

1. _____ True __√__ False   The Johnson family spends most of their time communicating with each other.

    _____

2. _____ True __√__ False   In the past, Americans spent less time with their families than they do today.

    _____

3. __√__ True _____ False   Families spend less time together as computers become more popular.

    _____

4. _____ True __√__ False   Surfing the Internet is usually done as a family.

    _____

5. __√__ True _____ False   More women feel ignored by family Internet users than men do.

    _____

6. __√__ True _____ False   Michael Gilbert thinks families should spend more time together.

    _____

7. __√__ True _____ False   Young people can stay connected to their friends all day because of technology.

    _____

8. _____ True __√__ False   Steven Cho has very little Internet access at college.

    _____

Reading Analysis

Read each question carefully. Circle the letter or the number of the correct answer, or write the answer in the space provided.

1. Read lines 1–3.
    a. What word is a synonym for **thrilled**?

    Excited

    b. **Having access to** something means
       1. you can use something easily.
       2. you can afford to buy something.
       3. you can find something easily.

2. Read line 3.
    a. **They're not as excited anymore** because
       1. their children don't enjoy the Internet.
       2. their children spend too much time on the Internet.
       3. their children like to communicate with each other.
    b. Who are **they**?
       1. Mr. and Mrs. Johnson
       2. The children
       3. The family
    c. **Anymore** means
       1. anyone.
       2. any longer.
       3. again.
    d. **They're not as excited anymore** means
       1. everyone is still very excited.
       2. they used to be excited, but now they're not.
       3. they want to be excited, but now they can't be.

3. In line 4, **complains** means
    a. talks negatively.
    b. talks happily.   _advirb – verb_
    c. talks quickly.

4. Read lines 5–8. **The Johnson family is not alone in this situation** means
    a. many other families have the same problem.
    b. the Johnson family has a lot of friends.
    c. Mr. and Mrs. Johnson like to be alone with their family.

5. Read lines 10–11: **When technology competes with family time, technology wins. Competes** means

    a. has a contest where one side wins and the other side loses.

    b. makes a decision about what is more important.

    c. has a problem that someone needs to solve.

6. Read lines 11–14.

    a. **Reduction** means

        1. increase.

        2. decrease.

    b. Who is Michael Gilbert?

        1. A friend of the Johnson family

        2. An Internet user

        3. A technology researcher

7. In lines 13–14, what word is a synonym for **boundless**?

    unlimited   unlimited

8. Read lines 16–17. **Interact** means

    a. communicate.

    b. have fun.

    c. get information.

9. Read lines 17–18. A **concern** is a

    a. kind of technology.

    b. worry.

    c. choice.

10. Read lines 19–20.

    a. What is the **significant difference** between television and the Internet?

        1. Families cannot use the Internet together, but they can watch TV together.

        2. Families cannot watch TV together, but they can use the Internet together.

        3. Families can watch TV and use the Internet together.

    b. **Significant** means

        1. new.

        2. important.

        3. popular.

11. In line 21, a **solitary activity** is
    a. something that you do with other people.
    b. something you do with your family.
    c. something you do alone.

12. Read this sentence: **Although they can help parents keep track of their children, cell phones also give children more privacy.**
    a. **Although** means
       1. also.
       2. even though.
       3. as a result.
    b. **Although** connects two ideas in a sentence. These ideas
       1. are both positive ideas.
       2. are both negative ideas.
       3. are one positive idea and one negative idea.
    c. When you have **privacy** using a cell phone,
       1. no one can find you.
       2. no one can call you.
       3. no one knows who is calling you.
    d. **They help parents keep track of their children** means
       1. parents can know where their children are.
       2. children can find their parents.
       3. cell phones give children a lot of privacy.

13. Read lines 27–32.
    a. **Families with higher incomes** are
       1. families who don't have a lot of money.
       2. families who make more money than other families make.
       3. families who have more important jobs than other people's jobs.
    b. **Women say that they feel ignored** means
       1. they feel that no one is helping them.
       2. they feel that they don't have enough time.
       3. they feel that no one is paying attention to them.

14. Read lines 41–42. **He is happy to have a break from it.**
    a. Who is **he**?
       1. Steven Cho
       2. Mr. Johnson
       3. Michael Gilbert

b. What is **it**?
1. The TV
2. The Internet
3. His college

c. **Have a break from** means
1. get away from.
2. get information from.
3. get tired of.

15. Read lines 42–43. **The Internet is here to stay, and so are cell phones** means
a. computers and cell phones stay in our homes.
b. someday people will not use cell phones and computers anymore.
c. people will always have cell phones and computers.

16. What is the main idea of the passage?
a. Family time decreases as technology becomes more popular.
b. Family time increases as technology becomes more popular.
c. Children have more privacy because of cell phones.

Vocabulary Skills

PART 1

Recognizing Word Forms

In English, the noun form and the verb form of some words are the same, for example, *research (n.)*, *research (v.).*

Complete each sentence with the correct word form on the left. Then circle *(v.)* if you are using a verb or *(n.)* if you are using a noun. Write all the verbs in the simple present in either the affirmative or the negative form. The nouns may be singular or plural.

access

1. Steven Cho _does not_ the Internet when he is at a camp in upstate New York.
   (v.) / (n.)

   He is happy that there is no _access_ to the Internet so that he can relax.
   (v.) / (n.)

Noun : singular / plural

verb : verb tenses / not

decrease   **2.** Some people believe that family time _decreases_ as technology increases.
                    (v.) / (n.)

Mrs. Johnson thinks that this _decrease_ in family time is not good for her family.
                    (v.) / (n.)

network   **3.** Most teenagers enjoy social _networks_, such as Facebook and Instagram.
                    (v.) / (n.)

They can easily _network_ with people all over the world.
                    (v.) / (n.)

contact   **4.** Our friends _they Contact_ us using technology any time they wish.
                    (v.) / (n.)

Because of technology, our social _contacts_ are always easy to reach.
                    (v.) / (n.)

concern   **5.** The Johnson children have a lot of privacy, and this _Concerns_ Mrs. Johnson.
                    (v.) / (n.)

However, this is not a _Concern_ for her children. They enjoy their privacy!
                    (v.) / (n.)

PART 2

Using a Dictionary

In English, words may have more than one meaning depending on the context. For example, *run* may refer to moving very fast (*Lee **runs** in several races every year.*). It may also mean operate or control (*Maria **runs** her own company.*). In addition, *run* can mean to try to get elected to something (*My friend is going to **run** for election as governor next year.*).

1. Read the following sentence. Use the context to help you understand the word in bold. Then read the dictionary entry for **drop** and circle the appropriate definition.

Gilbert reported that 35 percent of higher-income families felt there was a **drop** in face-to-face time.

> **drop** /drɑp/ *n.* **1** a very small amount of liquid: *I put a drop of medicine in my eye.* **2** a fall or a sharp movement down: *There was a 20-degree drop in the temperature last night.* **3** a distance down: *There's a 12-foot drop from that window.* **4** a delivery of supplies by parachute: *The plane made a food drop to the refugee camp.*

2. Circle the letter of the sentence that has the appropriate meaning of **drop**.

   a. Gilbert reported that 35 percent of higher-income families felt there was a small amount of liquid in face-to-face time.

   b. Gilbert reported that 35 percent of higher-income families felt there was sharp movement down in face-to-face time.

   c. Gilbert reported that 35 percent of higher-income families felt there was distance down in face-to-face time.

3. Which word is a synonym for **drop**?

   a. reduction
   b. distance
   c. movement

4. Read the following sentences. Use the context to help you understand the word in bold. Then read the dictionary entry for **situation** and circle the appropriate definition.

   "Our family spends more time surfing the Internet than communicating with each other," complains Mr. Johnson. The Johnson family is not alone in this **situation**.

   ---
   situation /ˌsɪtʃuˈeɪʃən/ *n*. **1** the way things are at a certain time, the state of what's happening: *The child was in a bad situation, with no food or water.* ‖ *The leaders are meeting to talk about the situation in the Middle East.* **2** *frml.* a job: *She no longer cleans house for us; she is looking for a different situation.* **3** a location, the way s.t. stands in its surroundings: *Our house's situation lets us look west over the desert.*

   ---

5. Circle the letter of the sentence that has the appropriate meaning of **situation**.

   a. The Johnson family is not alone in this job.
   b. The Johnson family is not alone in this location.
   c. The Johnson family is not alone in the way things are.

6. **Situation** means

   a. a place where people meet.
   b. the friends that you have.
   c. the way that things are.

Vocabulary in Context

Read the following sentences. Complete each sentence with the correct word from the box. Use each word only once.

although (adv.)	complains (v.)	significant (adj.)	solitary (adj.)
anymore (adv.)	interact (v.)	situation (n.)	thrilled (adj.)
competed (v.)	reduction (n.)		

1. Trudy is a very _solitary_ person. She enjoys spending most of her time alone.

2. Parents and children don't always _interact_ very well, especially if they don't talk with each other enough.

3. Olga was accepted to the university of her choice. She is _thrilled_!

4. Kubra moved to the United States from Germany with her family. They don't live in Germany _anymore_.

5. _although_ Juan has a big test tomorrow, he's going to a party tonight with Max.

6. Emily had to quickly move out of her house. Because of her _situation_, she is living with me until she finds a new apartment.

7. The students _competed_ to see who was the fastest runner in the school. Justin was very excited when he won the race.

8. After a holiday, there is often a big _reduction_ in prices. You can save a lot of money if you shop then.

9. Joshua spends a _competed_ amount of time surfing the Internet. He spends about eight hours a day online!

10. I don't enjoy spending time with Lisa. She always _complains_ about everything. She's a very negative person.

Compete — Competition

Complete — Finish

Reading Skill

Understanding a Venn Diagram

Venn diagrams show the differences and similarities between two topics. Using a Venn diagram can help you organize and understand important information from a reading passage.

Read the passage again, and then read the sentences below. Write the sentences in the Venn diagram.

- Children watched too much TV.
- Children spend too much time on the Internet.
- Families could watch TV together.
- Surfing the Internet is a solitary activity.
- Parents worry that families don't spend enough time together.
- Parents always knew who was calling their children on the phone.
- Children have too much privacy.

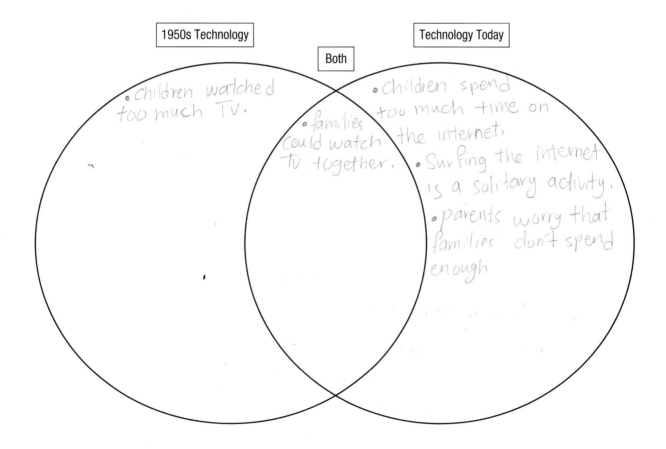

1950s Technology

Both

Technology Today

- Children watched too much TV.
- families could watch TV together.
- Children spend too much time on the internet.
- Surfing the internet is a solitary activity.
- parents worry that families don't spend enough

Information Recall

Read the passage again, and review the Venn diagram. Then answer the questions.

1. Why are Mr. and Mrs. Johnson unhappy about having a computer in their home?

   Family Time is reduced. the Kids spend more Time on The computer than interacting with their parents.

2. What is a negative result of the Internet's popularity?

   Less interaction with the family (in real life).

3. What is the biggest difference between technology in the 1950s and technology today?

   Tv-family could do it together internet/computer-it/a solitary activity.

Writing a Summary

A summary is a short paragraph that provides the most important information from a reading. It usually does not include details, just the main ideas. When you write a summary, it is important to use your own words, and not copy directly from the reading.

Write a brief summary of the passage. It should not be more than four sentences. Use your own words. The first two sentences of the summary are below. Write two more sentences to complete the summary.

> Some parents are unhappy that their children spend so much time on the Internet because it means spending less time together as a family. Research shows that families don't communicate as much when they have access to the Internet. _In recent years. Families are spending less time together although family time is important. Because of the internet, family members have more solitary activities._

Topics for Discussion and Writing

1. Teachers sometimes complain that students spend so much time with technology that they do not read books anymore. Teachers also say that students write less and are losing this skill. Do you agree with this? Why or why not?

2. People between the ages of 18 and 34 are often called millennials. Recent research shows that people in this age group are very connected to their mobile devices. Look at the graphic below and complete each sentence with the correct percentage.
   a. _____ percent of millennials would always return home to get their mobile device.
   b. _____ percent of millennials would travel 21 to 30 minutes to get their mobile device.
   c. _____ percent of millennials would travel 11 to 20 minutes to get their mobile device.
   d. _____ percent of millennials would travel 0–10 minutes to get their mobile device.
   e. _____ percent of millennials would never return home to get their mobile device.
   f. _____ percent of millennials would return home if they could get back in 20 minutes or less.

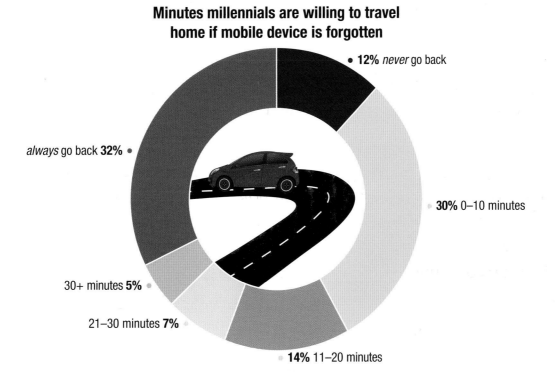

Minutes millennials are willing to travel home if mobile device is forgotten

- **12%** *never* go back
- *always* go back **32%**
- **30%** 0–10 minutes
- 30+ minutes **5%**
- 21–30 minutes **7%**
- **14%** 11–20 minutes

Credit: USC Annenberg Center for the Digital Future and Bovitz, Inc.

3. Look at the pie chart again. How far would you travel to get your mobile device? Discuss this question with a partner. Then, with your class, compile your answers in a chart on the board. How far would most of your classmates travel to get their mobile devices?

4. Write in your journal. What effects has technology had on your life? How has it improved your life? Has technology had any negative effects on your life? Explain.

Critical Thinking

1. Look at the chart below, and then read the following sentences. Circle the letter of each sentence that is true.
   a. Most people prefer to get their news from television.
   b. Most people prefer to get their news from the Internet.
   c. Few people prefer to get their news from the radio.
   d. More people aged 65 and older get their news from newspapers than any other group.
   e. More people aged 50–64 get their news from the Internet than people 30–49 years old.

Preferred News Sources by Age Group in the United States

Source	18–29	30–49	50–64	65+
Television	50%	50%	58%	68%
Internet	27%	28%	18%	6%
Newspaper/Magazine	7%	6%	8%	18%
Radio	3%	7%	7%	4%
Other	6%	6%	5%	2%
No opinion	7%	2%	3%	3%

Source: http://www.gallup.com/poll/163412/americans-main-source-news.aspx

2. Work with a partner. Look at the items in the box. Which of these things are most important to you and your partner? Put them in order on the chart on page 47. #1 is the most important and #7 is the least important. Then compare your answers.

automobile	cell phone	home computer	tablet
cable or satellite TV	high-speed Internet	iPod	

Your Answers	Your Partner's Answers
1.	1.
2.	2.
3.	3.
4.	4.
5.	5.
6.	6.
7.	7.

3. In the reading passage, Michael Gilbert says, "It can't be a good thing that families are spending less face-to-face time together." Do you agree with him? Why or why not? What do you think happens when families spend less time together? Discuss these questions with your classmates.

4. Some people say that they communicate more with technology because they talk frequently on their cell phones, send e-mail and text messages, and use social networks. Think about this question: What are the advantages and disadvantages of communicating electronically with others, instead of communicating face-to-face? Talk about this question with a partner. Then compare your answers with your classmates' answers.

Crossword Puzzle

Review the words in the box below. Then read the clues on the next page. Write the words in the correct spaces in the puzzle.

access	complain	interact	significant
although	concern	network	situation
anymore	drop	privacy	solitary
break	excited	reduction	thrilled
compete	ignore		

Crossword Puzzle Clues

ACROSS CLUES

3. We are very _excited_ because we have new computer games.

5. Parents often _complain_ that their children spend too much time on the Internet.

6. You need to put in a password to get _access_ to your e-mail.

8. Many American families spend less time together these days. Many families in other countries are in the same _situation_ too.

9. When Anna wants _privacy_, she closes the door to her room.

10. There has been a large _reduction_ in the number of people who use traditional telephones. Most people use cell phones today.

12. Surfing the Internet is often a _solitary_ activity. Many people do it alone.

14. Facebook is an example of a social _network_.

17. No one uses videotapes _anymore_. They are out of date.

18. I'm _thrilled_ about my new cell phone. It can do so much more than my old one!

DOWN CLUES

1. There is a _significant_ difference between putting information on Facebook and talking face-to-face with your friends.

2. Researchers expect to see a _drop_ in the amount of time families spend together over the next several years.

4. Can family time _compete_ successfully with the Internet, or will the Internet win?

7. Some people share a _concern_ that children don't get enough exercise because they're at their computers too much.

11. Parents and children need to _interact_ with each other, especially at dinnertime. That's a good time to talk!

13. _although_ Toby is only three years old, he already knows how to use a cell phone!

15. Some people have dinner together in a restaurant, but they _ignore_ each other and talk on their cell phones to other people.

16. I am tired. I need a _break_ from the computer. I'm going for a walk.

Issues in Today's Society

Young people on escalators

1. How is society today different than in the past? Give examples and explain.

2. Are children today the same as children 50 years ago? Why or why not?

3. What are some important issues in society now?

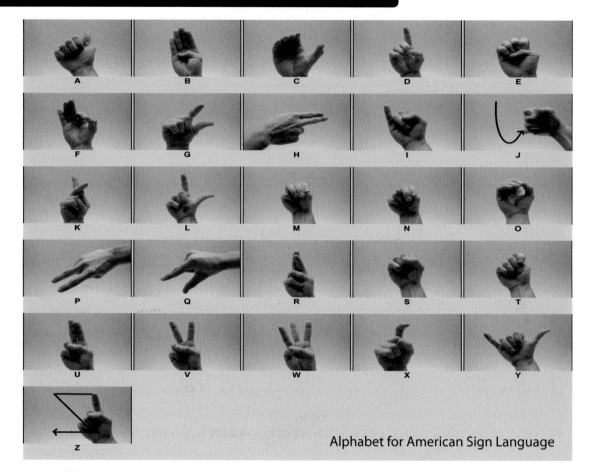

Alphabet for American Sign Language

Prereading

1. What is language?
   a. Work with two classmates and write a definition of the word *language*.
   b. Write your group's definition of *language* on the board. Compare your definition with your classmates' definitions.
   c. Create a single definition of *language* with your class and write it on the board.

2. At what age do most babies learn to speak? How do they learn to speak?

3. How do you think deaf babies learn to communicate?

4. How do deaf people communicate?

5. Look at the alphabet for American Sign Language on page 52. Who uses it, and why?
   a. In groups of three, use the sign language chart to learn to "sign" an object in the room—for example, *chair* or *pen*.
   b. Sign your word to your classmates, and they will say the name of the object.

6. Read the title of this chapter. Reread your definitions of *language*. Do you think human language must be spoken? Is there any other way that people can communicate?

Reading

🎧 **Read the passage carefully. Then complete the exercises that follow.**

CD 1
TR 5

Sign Language for Everyone

1   Most of us know a little about how babies learn to talk. From the time infants are
2   born, they hear language because their parents talk to them all the time. Between the
3   ages of seven and ten months, most infants begin to make sounds. They repeat the
4   same sounds over and over again. For example, a baby may repeat the sound *dadada*
5   or *bababa*. This activity is called babbling. When babies babble, they are practicing
6   language. Soon, the sound *dadada* may become *daddy*, and *bababa* may become *bottle*.
7   What happens, though, to children who cannot hear? How do deaf children learn
8   to communicate? Recently, doctors have learned that deaf babies babble with their
9   hands. Laura-Ann Petitto, a psychologist at Gallaudet University in Washington,
10 D.C., has studied how children learn language. She observed three hearing infants
11 and two deaf infants. The three hearing infants had English-speaking parents. The
12 two deaf infants had deaf mothers and fathers who used American Sign Language
13 (ASL) to communicate with each other and with their babies. Dr. Petitto studied the
14 babies three times: at 10, 12, and 14 months. During this time, children really begin to
15 develop their language skills.
16 Dr. Petitto and her assistants studied the children for four months and made many
17 important observations. For instance, they saw that the hearing children made many
18 different, varied motions with their hands. However, there appeared to be no pattern
19 to these motions. The deaf babies also made many different movements with their
20 hands. However, the deaf babies' movements were more consistent, and they seemed
21 to prefer certain hand shapes. In fact, during the four-month period, the deaf babies'
22 hand motions started to resemble some of the basic hand shapes used in ASL.
23 Hearing infants start with simple syllable babbling (*dadada*), and then put more
24 syllables together to sound like real sentences and questions. Apparently, deaf babies
25 follow this same pattern, too. First, they repeat simple hand shapes. Next, they form
26 simple hand signs (words) and use these movements together to resemble ASL sentences.

27 Linguists—people who study language—believe that our ability for language is
28 innate. In other words, humans are born with the capacity for language. It does not
29 matter if we are physically able to speak or not.

30 Other researchers have begun additional studies that focus on teaching "baby
31 signs" to hearing infants. Baby signs are simple signs to help hearing babies
32 communicate more easily when they are too young to speak, for example, *mom*, *dad*,
33 *cold*, *hungry*, *tired*. Researchers at the National Institute of Health (NIH) conducted
34 a study to compare two groups of 11-month-old hearing babies. They taught some
35 simple baby signs to the first group, and focused on verbal, or speech, training to the
36 second group. Surprisingly, by the time the hearing babies who learned baby signs
37 were two years old, they were more advanced talkers than the second group.

38 The spoken language difference between the two groups continued to grow. The
39 babies who learned sign language spoke better at three years old, too. Researchers
40 tested the children again at eight years old, and there was still a difference. The
41 researchers have concluded that teaching signs to hearing babies improves their
42 verbal development.

43 Because of the study's positive results, researchers now want to focus on early
44 infant education. Although these studies are new, researchers believe teaching baby
45 signs can be very helpful to all children.

A mother and child communicating with sign language

Fact Finding

Read the passage again. Then read the following statements. Check (√) whether each statement is True or False. If a statement is false, rewrite it so that it is true. Then go back to the passage and find the line that supports your answer.

1. _____ True _____ False   Most infants start to babble after they are a year old.

   _____

2. _____ True _____ False   Dr. Petitto studied only deaf babies.

   _____

3. _____ True _____ False   Dr. Petitto saw that deaf babies and hearing babies moved their hands the same way.

   _____

4. _____ True _____ False   Linguists believe that we are all born with the ability for language.

   _____

5. _____ True _____ False   NIH researchers taught baby signs to hearing babies and deaf babies.

   _____

6. _____ True _____ False   The hearing babies who learned baby signs became better talkers than the group that did not learn baby signs.

   _____

7. _____ True _____ False   Researchers believe that teaching baby signs improves verbal development.

   _____

Reading Analysis

Read each question carefully. Circle the letter or the number of the correct answer, or write the answer in the space provided.

1. Read lines 1–5.
   a. Which word is a synonym for **infants**?

   bybies

   b. What is **babbling**?

   the baby mahing a socinds lihe dadda.

2. Read lines 8–14.
   a. **Deaf** people
      1. can hear.
      2. cannot hear.
   b. **Observe** means
      1. see and notice.
      2. communicate with.
      3. compare with.
   c. What is **ASL**?

   American sine Language

   d. Who uses ASL? Why?

   People who deaf

3. Read lines 17–22.
   a. **For instance** means
      1. however.
      2. so that.
      3. for example.
   b. What are **varied motions**?
      1. Different sounds
      2. Different movements
      3. Different signs
   c. **Consistent** means
      1. careful or helpful.
      2. unchanging or steady.
      3. common or normal.
   d. What is the purpose of **in fact**?
      1. To give true information
      2. To emphasize the previous information
      3. To introduce different information

e. **Resemble** means
   1. look exactly like.
   2. be similar to.
   3. make movements like.

f. Which of the following statements are true? Check (√) all that apply.
   1. ✓ All children make motions with their hands.
   2. ✗ Only the deaf children made many different movements with their hands.
   3. ✗ The hearing children's hand movements had a pattern.
   4. ✓ The deaf children's hand movements had a pattern.

g. Complete the following sentence correctly.

   Both the deaf and the hearing children made movements with their hands, but

   1. they all made the same movements over and over again.
   2. only the deaf children repeated the same hand motions.
   3. only the hearing children repeated the same hand motions.

4. Read lines 21–22. "**During the four-month period, the deaf babies' hand motions started to resemble some of the basic hand shapes used in ASL.**" This sentence means that
   a. the deaf babies were studying ASL.
   b. the deaf babies were repeating their parents' hand signs.
   c. the deaf babies stopped babbling.

5. Read lines 23–25. **Apparently** means
   a. strangely.
   b. simply.
   c. clearly.

6. Read lines 28–30: "**Linguists**—people who study language—believe that our ability for language is **innate. In other words**, humans are born with the capacity for language."
   a. What is a **linguist**?

   People who study

   b. How do you know?

   c. **Innate** describes
     1. something you are born with.
     2. something you are able to do.
     3. something a linguist does.

   d. What follows **in other words**?
     1. A new idea
     2. An explanation of the previous idea
     3. An example of the previous idea

7. Read lines 31–34. **Baby signs** are

    a. ASL for deaf children.

    b. simple signs to help all babies communicate.

    c. a new kind of research.

8. Read lines 35–38. **Verbal training** means

    a. teaching the children to speak.

    b. teaching the children baby signs.

    c. teaching the children to hear.

9. Read lines 41–42. **Concluded** means

    a. seen a difference.

    b. done research.

    c. formed an opinion.

10. What is the main idea of the passage?

    a. Both deaf children and hearing children learn to communicate in similar ways at about the same time.

    b. Children begin to develop their language skills at around two years of age.

    c. Many linguists believe that all humans are born with the ability to speak.

Vocabulary Skills

PART 1

Recognizing Word Forms

In English, there are several ways that adjectives change to nouns. Some adjectives become nouns by changing the final -t to -ce, for example, *ignorant (adj.)*, *ignorance (n.)*.

Complete each sentence with the correct word form on the left. The nouns may be singular or plural.

A **important** *(adj.)*   **1.** Dr. Petitto and her assistants are studying the _____B_____ of babbling

B **importance** *(n.)*   for all children. She and her assistants made many __A__

             observations when they studied deaf and hearing infants.

                          babe

A different *(adj.)*

B difference *(n.)*

2. The hearing children made many __A__ movements with their hands. There were many __B__ in the hand movements of the deaf and hearing children.

A significant *(adj.)*

B significance *(n.)*

3. Researchers are studying the __B__ of teaching baby signs to hearing infants. The children who learn baby signs show __A__ improvement in their speech.

A dependent *(adj.)*

B dependence *(n.)*

4. As the hearing children grew up, their __B__ on baby signs decreased. However, deaf children are __A__ on sign language.

A persistent *(adj.)*

B persistence *(n.)*

5. The deaf babies in Dr. Petitto's study were very __A__. Their different hand motions slowly changed to ASL hand shapes because of their __B__.

PART 2

Using a Dictionary

In English, words may have more than one meaning, depending on the context. For example, *change* may refer to becoming something different (*We changed our lives by moving from a city to a small town.*). It may also mean make something different (*We changed the color of our living room from blue to yellow.*). In addition, *change* can mean to convert money (*The tourists changed U.S. dollars into Japanese yen.*).

1. Read the following sentences. Use the context to help you understand the word in bold. Then read the dictionary entry for **pattern** and circle the appropriate definition.

They saw that the hearing children made many different, varied motions with their hands. However, there appeared to be no **pattern** to these motions.

Pupil
↓
shdenT

> **pattern** /ˈpætərn/ *n.* **1** an example or model to be followed: *A research paper must follow a specific pattern.* **2** a form or guide to follow when making s.t.: *She made the dress herself from a pattern.* **3** a design of regular shapes and lines: *The flower pattern in that dress is very pretty.* **4** a repeated set of events, characteristics, or features: *There is a pattern to his behavior, in that he grows quiet when he's sad.*

2. Circle the letter of the sentence that has the appropriate meaning of **pattern**.

    a. There appeared to be no example or model to follow in these motions.

    b. There appeared to be no repeated set of characteristics in these motions.

    c. There appeared to be no design of regular shapes and lines in these motions.

    d. There appeared to be no form or guide to follow in these motions.

3. A **pattern** of motions is

    a. an observation of movements.

    b. a reason for movements.

    c. a repeated set of movements.

4. Read the following sentence. Use the context to help you understand the word in bold. Then read the dictionary entry for **capacity**. Circle the appropriate definition.

    The **capacity** for language is uniquely human.

                only for

> **capacity** /kəˈpæsəti/ *n.* **-ties 1** *sing.* [U] the ability to contain, hold, or absorb: *That restaurant has a 100-seat capacity.* **2** *sing.* [U] the greatest amount that s.t. can contain, the maximum volume: *There is no more room in the bottle; it is filled to capacity.* **3** [C;U] the ability to do s.t.: *He has the capacity to work long hours.* **4** [C;U] the power to learn and remember knowledge: *She has a great capacity for learning.* **5** [C] the power that goes with a certain position or role: *She signs the company checks in her capacity as owner.* **6** [U] the best or maximum amount of production: *That factory is working at capacity.*

5. Circle the letter of the sentence that has the appropriate meaning of **capacity**.

    a. The greatest amount of language that can be contained is uniquely human.

    b. The ability to contain or hold language is uniquely human.

    c. The power to learn and remember language is uniquely human.

6. **Capacity** means

    a. language.

    b. ability.

    c. belief.

Vocabulary in Context

Read the following sentences. Complete each sentence with the correct word or phrase from the box. Use each word or phrase only once.

apparently *(adv.)*	for instance	motion *(n.)*	resemble *(v.)*
capacity *(n.)*	in other words	observe *(v.)*	varied *(adj.)*
consistent *(adj.)*	innate *(adj.)*		

1. It's getting dark and there are a lot of clouds in the sky. appar _____, it's going to rain this afternoon.

2. I _____ my mother. We are both very tall and have blue eyes and curly blond hair.

3. Animals do not have the _____ for speech. Only humans can communicate with words.

4. Henry has a _____ life. During the day, he is a student. In the evenings, he works as a waiter. On Saturdays, he teaches swimming to children, and on Sundays, he sings in a choir.

5. Researchers are trained to carefully _____ everything. They need to learn what to look for and how to record what they see.

6. Human babies have many _____ abilities. Walking and speaking are two of them.

7. In different cultures, the same _____, such as waving your hand, may have different meanings.

8. Janet complains about everything. She's always too warm or too cold. She doesn't like anything. _____, Janet is a very negative person.

9. Matthew enjoys going out to restaurants to experience the food of different cultures. _____, last weekend he went to an Indian restaurant. Tomorrow night, he will try Japanese food.

10. Our homework assignment is _____ in this class. Every week we must study ten new vocabulary words and write them in sentences.

Reading Skill

Using Headings to Create an Outline

Readings often have headings. Headings introduce new ideas or topics. They also introduce details. Using headings to make an outline can help you understand and remember the most important information from the reading.

شعور بالوحدة
Loneliness

وحيد
Lonely

الوحدة
Alone

Use the sentences below to complete the outline.

1 • They focused on verbal skills with the second group.

2 • Teaching baby signs to hearing babies can improve their verbal development.

3 • They studied two groups of 11-month-old hearing babies.

4 • She studied three hearing infants and two deaf infants.

5 • They taught baby signs to the first group.

6 • The sounds become words.

7 • She studied them three times: at 10, 12, and 14 months.

8 • They make many different movements with their hands, but they make the same movements over and over again.

I. How Babies Learn Language

    A. Hearing Babies

        1. <u>Between the ages of seven and ten months, they begin to babble, or make the same sounds over and over again.</u>

        2. _____6_____

    B. Deaf Babies

        1. _____8_____

        2. <u>The hand motions start to resemble some of the basic hand shapes used in ASL.</u>

II. Dr. Petitto's Research on How Babies Learn Language

    A. Who did she study?

        _____4_____

    B. How did she study them?

        _____7_____

    C. Conclusion:

    <u>The hearing children made varied motions with their hands, but the deaf babies made the same hand movements over and over again.</u>

III. National Institute of Health Research on Baby Signs

    A. Who did they study?

        3

    B. How did they study the children?

       Group 1:

        5

       Group 2:

        1

    C. Results:

        2

Information Recall

Read the passage again, and review the outline. Then answer the questions.

    1. What did Dr. Petitto learn about deaf and hearing children?

       line 9 to 26

    2. What did the researchers at the NIH learn?

       line 33 To 42

    3. As a result of all the research, what do researchers believe?

       C

Writing a Summary

A summary is a short paragraph that provides the most important information from a reading. It usually does not include details, just the main ideas. When you write a summary, it is important to use your own words, and not copy directly from the reading.

Write a brief summary of the passage. It should not be more than four sentences. Use your own words. The first two sentences of the summary have been written for you. Write two more sentences to complete the summary.

Most babies learn to talk by making and repeating sounds, which eventually become words.

Dr. Petitto discovered that deaf babies start making hand shapes, which also eventually become signs and even ASL sentences.

Topics for Discussion and Writing

1. Many famous people of the past and present have been deaf. Despite their disability, they were successful in their lives. For example, Helen Keller was an important author and scholar, and Marlee Matlin is a famous American actress. Write about a famous person or someone you know who was or is hearing-impaired (deaf) or has another kind of disability. Tell about what that person has accomplished in spite of his or her disability.

2. Sign language is one important form of nonverbal communication. Can you think of another type of nonverbal communication? Describe it.

3. What do you think about teaching "baby signs" to hearing children before they can speak? Do you think it is useful? Why or why not?

4. Write in your journal. Is it important for you to learn sign language? Why or why not?

Preschool children learning
sign language in class

Critical Thinking

1. Doctors have developed a controversial operation (a cochlear implant) to enable deaf people to "hear." Many deaf people are opposed to this operation. They say that they are not really disabled. They feel they are a minority group and should be accepted as they are—non-hearing people. They feel it is wrong to force children to have this operation and that the operation does not really enable the deaf to hear as well as non-deaf people do anyway. They feel that their sign language should be accepted in the same way as any spoken language.

   Work in a group of four students. Make a list of the advantages and disadvantages of remaining deaf (and not having the operation) and a list of the advantages and disadvantages of having the operation. Next to your lists of advantages and disadvantages, write the consequences of remaining deaf and the consequences of being able to "hear." Compare your lists with your classmates' lists.

2. Many deaf people feel that ASL is a real language. They believe that hearing people should learn it just as they learn other languages. The alphabet for American Sign Language on page 52 is only for spelling out words, letter by letter. Go online and find a website for learning ASL. In small groups, learn to "sign" some basic words and sentences. Then, in your group, discuss what it may be like for a hearing person to learn ASL compared to learning a spoken language. Discuss your conclusions with your classmates.

3. Doctors learned that deaf babies "babble" with their hands. Why do you think the children do this?

4. Dr. Petitto studied the babies at 10, 12, and 14 months. Why do you think she studied them so often? Discuss this with a partner.

Crossword Puzzle

Review the words in the box below. Then read the clues on the next page. Write the words in the correct spaces in the puzzle.

apparently	consistent	linguist	resemble
ASL	deaf	motions	training
babbling	infant	observe	varied
capacity	innate	pattern	verbal
conclude			

Crossword Puzzle Clues

ACROSS CLUES

8. Researchers _____ deaf and hearing children and make note of their behavior.

9. Children receive _____ in sign language. They learn it from a teacher.

10. A person who cannot hear is _____.

13. Children copy what they hear and see. _____, this is the way they learn to speak and to sign.

15. A baby is a(n) _____.

17. When children begin to make _____ movements with their hands, researchers can see that they have learned hand signs.

DOWN CLUES

1. As deaf babies develop, the _____ of their hand movements becomes very regular.

2. Children's ability to speak is their _____ ability.

3. _____ are movements.

4. A _____ is a person who studies language.

5. Researchers _____ from their studies that verbal and nonverbal "speech" are both true languages.

6. Deaf children's hand motions _____, or are similar to, the hand signals of ASL.

7. Our _____, or ability, to communicate is something we are born with.

11. All babies make _____, or different, movements with their hands.

12. _____ refers to the repeated sounds that babies make.

14. The ability to fly is a(n) _____ ability in most birds.

16. _____ is the abbreviation for American Sign Language.

Children playing in a park

Prereading

1. What do you think of as a happy childhood? What should children be doing after school, on weekends, and during the summer?

2. Discuss your childhood. What was it like? Did you have fun playing with your friends? Did you spend a lot of after-school time studying?

3. If you have children, or plan to have children, what kind of childhood is best for them? Why do you think so?

4. Read the title of the chapter. What do you think this chapter is about?

A young girl learning to use a laptop computer

Reading

🎧 **Read the passage carefully. Then complete the exercises that follow.**

CD 1
TR 6

Our kids are growing up too fast!

1   I am an adult with many responsibilities, which can cause a lot of stress in my
2 life. When I am having a really bad day, I sometimes think to myself, "It would be
3 so nice to be a child again and not have all this stress!" My childhood was fun and
4 carefree most of the time. After school, my friends and I got together and played
5 until dinnertime without any adults around. We walked or rode our bicycles to each
6 other's homes. We used our imaginations to invent new games. Sometimes we just
7 sat under a tree and daydreamed. We even got into mischief at times, although it
8 was never anything serious. We were kids!
9   But childhood today is different. Many children have a lot of stress in their lives
10 and pressure to succeed. Our culture today emphasizes success, and this starts in
11 childhood. "It's a difficult time for parents because there are so many pressures
12 from society that are unhealthy," says Dr. David Elkind, author of *The Hurried Child*:
13 *Growing Up Too Fast*. Many children learn to use computers and tablets before they
14 can walk. Some learn to read and count before they go to nursery school. There is a
15 much greater emphasis today on academic achievement than in the past. As a result,
16 they have tutors and attend study classes after school to help them to compete
17 with other children. Many parents worry that if they don't enroll their kids in a
18 lot of after-school activities, such as music classes or soccer, their children will be
19 left behind. Sometimes, though, parents involve their children in so many outside
20 activities that they really have very little time left just to play, have fun, and be

21 kids. It seems that society rushes them to grow up too quickly. We have to ask the
22 question, "Are kids growing up too fast these days?" This rush through childhood
23 can cause the same kinds of stress in children that adults have.

24   It's difficult for children to do well in school when they feel too much pressure to
25 succeed. Dr. Elkind advises parents to let children be children. In other words, parents
26 should let children act like children. His research suggests that students are more likely
27 to have academic success if their parents do not hurry them through their childhood.
28 Dr. Elkind believes that play is an important part of childhood. It's important for
29 children to play with others to reduce stress, develop creativity, and experience joy.

30   There are many other reasons why children should not grow up too fast. Childhood
31 gives children the time they need to mature and learn important lessons. They need
32 time to develop relationships. Elkind says, "A big part of childhood is being able to
33 spend time playing with peers." Peers are people our age. "This is very important
34 because it gives children the opportunity to learn about themselves. They learn
35 respect and how to work with others, too." Childhood is also a time when kids learn
36 how to enjoy themselves. "Play gives children a sense of enjoyment that they can call
37 upon later in life," says Elkind. "When they're adults and feeling down or stressed,
38 they can remember those happy, carefree times when they were children."

39   Childhood experiences give us the happy memories that we can think about when
40 we're adults. If we rush our kids to grow up, they won't have the chance to make
41 happy memories like the ones I recall from my own childhood.

Fact Finding

Read the passage again. Then read the following statements. Check (√) whether each statement is True or False. If a statement is false, rewrite it so that it is true. Then go back to the passage and find the line that supports your answer.

1. _____ True _____ False   The author had a lot of stress when she was a child.

   _____

2. _____ True _____ False   Children who have a lot of after-school activities are carefree.

   _____

3. _____ True _____ False   Many children today have the same kinds of stress as adults have.

   _____

4. _____ True _____ False   Children today have a lot of pressure to be successful.

   _____

5. _____ True _____ False   Dr. Elkind believes it's healthy for children to act like children.

_____

6. _____ True _____ False   Dr. Elkind says that children who rush through childhood have more academic success.

_____

7. _____ True _____ False   It's important for children to spend time with their peers.

_____

8. _____ True _____ False   Children have happy memories of childhood when they grow up very fast.

_____

Reading Analysis

Read each question carefully. Circle the letter or the number of the correct answer, or write the answer in the space provided.

1. What was the author's childhood like?
   a. The author never studied or did schoolwork, and was a poor student.
   b. The author had a very happy childhood, with time to play with friends.
   c. The author had music lessons and sports after school, and was very busy.

2. Read lines 1–5.
   a. **Stress** means
      1. responsibility.
      2. work.
      3. worries.
   b. **Childhood** refers to
      1. the period from birth to about 12 years old.
      2. the time when children are students.
      3. the time when children are not in school.
   c. When you are **carefree**, you
      1. do not study.
      2. have no worries.
      3. do not work.
   d. In the past, when children played after school,
      1. their parents watched what they were doing.
      2. their parents did not watch what they were doing.

3. Read lines 5–8.

   a. **Imagination** refers to

      1. your ability to be creative.

      2. your ability to play.

      3. your ability to make toys.

   b. When you **invent** something, you

      1. play a game.

      2. build something.

      3. create something new.

   c. **Mischief** refers to

      1. harmful activities that are serious.

      2. annoying activities that are not serious.

      3. dangerous activities that are serious.

4. Read lines 9–12. Many children have a lot of stress in their lives and **pressure to succeed**. Our culture today **emphasizes** success, and this starts in childhood.

   a. **Pressure to succeed** means to have

      1. a stressful feeling that you must be successful.

      2. an ability to be successful.

      3. a difficult childhood.

   b. **Emphasizes** means

      1. likes very much.

      2. places importance on something.

      3. thinks a lot about.

   c. These sentences mean that

      1. children today are more successful than children in the past were.

      2. our culture today helps children to be more successful.

      3. children today have a lot of stress because society expects them to be successful.

5. Read lines 11–18.

   a. Dr. David Elkind believes that

      1. children should spend time learning as much as possible from the time they are very small.

      2. it is unhealthy for children to spend so much time learning as much as possible from the time they are very small.

   b. **Academic achievement** is

      1. success in school.

      2. a carefree childhood.

      3. after-school activities.

   c. A **tutor** is a person who

      1. gives study classes for groups of students after school.

      2. teaches nursery school children how to count and read.

      3. teaches a student individually, usually after school.

     d. **Compete** means

       1. work with others to achieve something.

       2. try to do better than someone else.

       3. study hard to pass exams.

     e. **Enroll** means

       1. help.

       2. show.

       3. register.

6. **Many parents worry that if they don't enroll their kids in a lot of after-school activities, such as music classes or soccer, their children will be left behind.**

   This sentence means that

   a. some parents enjoy enrolling their kids in a lot of activities.

   b. some children want to do better than other children.

   c. some parents are afraid that other children will be better than their children.

7. Read lines 22–23. **Rush** means

   a. do something too quickly.

   b. never have any fun.

   c. grow up too fast.

8. Read lines 24–29.

     a. **Advises** means

       1. applies pressure.

       2. asks questions.

       3. gives suggestions.

     b. Which word in these lines is a synonym for **rush** in line 21?

       _____

     c. **Reduce** means

       1. get rid of.

       2. decrease.

       3. learn about.

     d. **Joy** means

       1. happiness.

       2. success.

       3. creativity.

9. Read lines 30–35.

     a. When you **mature**, you

       1. learn lessons.

       2. compete with others.

       3. grow up emotionally.

b. Your **peers** are
   1. other students in your school.
   2. people your own age.
   3. teachers and tutors.
c. **Opportunity** means
   1. ability.
   2. chance.
   3. reason.

10. Read lines 35–38. Which word is a synonym of **recall**?

_____

11. What is the main idea of the passage?
   a. Childhood in the past was different from childhood today.
   b. Children today experience a lot pressure and stress and are losing the chance for a real childhood.
   c. Children today work much harder at schoolwork than children in the past did.

Vocabulary Skills

PART 1

Recognizing Word Forms

In English, there are several ways that verbs change to nouns. Some verbs become nouns by adding the suffix -ment, for example, agree (v.), agreement (n.).

Complete each sentence with the correct word form on the left. Use the simple present of the verb in either the affirmative or the negative form. All the nouns are singular.

achieve *(v.)*   **1.** The _____ of academic success is important in society today.

achievement *(n.)*   Some children _____ this success by taking study classes

after school.

develop *(v.)*   **2.** Dr. Elkind believes that children today _____ important

development *(n.)*   relationships in childhood because they are too busy. This can be very

harmful to their _____.

enjoy *(v.)*	**3.** Some children _____ their childhoods because they are
enjoyment *(n.)*	always studying their schoolwork. However, they may need a sense
	of _____ later on in life.
enroll *(v.)*	**4.** Children don't always have time to play because of their _____ in
enrollment *(n.)*	after-school activities. Their parents often _____ them in music
	classes or sports.
involve *(v.)*	**5.** Some parents _____ children in too many activities. Their
involvement *(n.)*	_____ stops them from having a carefree childhood.

PART 2

Synonyms
Synonyms are words with similar meanings. For example, *success* and *achievement* are synonyms.

Match each word or phrase with its synonym. Write the letter of the correct answer and the word or phrase in the space provided.

i. without worries	1. carefree		a.	annoying activities
_____	2. enroll		b.	create
_____	3. invent		c.	decrease
_____	4. joy		d.	happiness
_____	5. mischief		e.	hurry
_____	6. pressure		f.	register
_____	7. recall		g.	remember
_____	8. reduce		h.	stress
_____	9. rush		i.	~~without worries~~

Vocabulary in Context

Read the following sentences. Complete each sentence with the correct word from the box. Use each word only once.

advises *(v.)*	emphasis *(n.)*	opportunity *(n.)*	rushed *(v.)*
childhood *(n.)*	imagination *(n.)*	peers *(n.)*	stress *(n.)*
competed *(v.)*	mature *(v.)*		

1. My sister is an excellent cook. She uses her _____ to create new, unusual dishes for our family.

2. Andy woke up late this morning, so he _____ to the bus stop. He wanted to be on time for his class.

3. I had a wonderful _____. I spent a lot of time playing with my friends.

4. Marco _____ in a race and won first place!

5. Our teacher _____ us to speak English outside of the classroom. I think it's a good suggestion.

6. The _____ in our reading class is on learning new vocabulary.

7. Children _____ as they grow up and develop relationships with their friends.

8. Most adults have a lot of _____ in their lives because of their work and responsibilities.

9. It's important for children to play with their _____. This helps them learn to respect other people.

10. I really enjoy my English classes because I have the _____ to speak with my classmates.

Reading Skill

Organizing Information in a Chart

It is important to be able to create charts. Charts can help you organize and understand information that you read.

Read the passage again. Complete the chart below.

	Description	After-School Activities	Things Children Learn
Childhood in the Past		Examples:	Examples:
Childhood Today		Examples:	Examples:

Information Recall

Read the passage again, and review the chart. Then answer the questions.

1. What was the author's life like as a child?

2. What are children's lives like today?

3. Why does Dr. Elkind advise parents to "let children be children"?

Writing a Summary

A summary is a short paragraph that provides the most important information from a reading. It usually does not include details, just the main ideas. When you write a summary, it is important to use your own words, and not copy directly from the reading.

Write a brief summary of the passage. The summary should not be more than four sentences. Use your own words. Be sure to indent the first line.

Topics for Discussion and Writing

1. Why do you think society today emphasizes academic success for children at a young age? Give some reasons.

2. Many people believe that children grow up too fast. What do you think are some reasons for this? Discuss this question with a partner and compare your ideas with your classmates' ideas.

3. How is childhood today different from when you were a child? Give examples. Talk about this with your classmates.

4. Write in your journal. Think about a carefree time in your childhood. How did you feel? Write about this and describe your experience.

Critical Thinking

1. Discuss these questions with a partner: Did you have a lot of pressure to succeed in school when you were a child? Do you think this is healthy for children? Why or why not?

2. Do you put a lot of pressure on yourself now to do well academically? Why or why not?

Crossword Puzzle

Review the words in the box below. Then read the clues on the next page. Write the words in the correct spaces in the puzzle.

advise	enroll	mischief	reduce
carefree	imagination	peers	rush
childhood	invent	pressure	stress
compete	joy	recall	tutor
emphasize	mature		

Crossword Puzzle Clues

ACROSS CLUES

3. As children grow up, they _____ and develop into adults.

5. Parents often _____, or register, their children for after-school programs and for sports.

8. Children learn from their parents and teachers, but they also learn from their _____. Their friends teach them a lot.

10. Was your _____ a happy one? Did you have fun as a kid?

13. Curious children often get into _____, but it's not harmful. It's part of growing up.

14. Some children _____ new games, or new rules for old games.

15. If parents and teachers put too much _____ on children to succeed, the children may become worried and unhappy.

16. These children have a _____ to help them with math after school.

17. Worrying about exams can cause a lot of _____.

18. There can be a lot of _____ in childhood if children have time for play.

DOWN CLUES

1. Small children need a _____ life. They shouldn't have to worry about succeeding.

2. What do you _____ from your childhood? Do you remember the games you used to play?

4. Parents _____ the importance of studying hard and doing well on exams.

6. Dr. Elkind believes that adults should not _____ children into growing up too fast.

7. Most children have a very lively _____. They create many interesting ways to play.

9. I _____ you to give your child some time to play. She studies too hard.

11. Students often _____ for awards, such as awards for best science project.

12. Adults can _____ the stress children have by giving them free time for play.

Prereading

1. What is *loneliness*?

2. Are *loneliness* and being *alone* the same? Explain your answer.

3. Work with a partner and make a list of some reasons why people may feel lonely. Write them in the chart on page 83. Have you or your partner ever felt lonely for these reasons? Circle your answers. Then discuss them with your partner.

Why do some people feel lonely?	You	Your Partner
	yes / no	yes / no
	yes / no	yes / no
	yes / no	yes / no
	yes / no	yes / no
	yes / no	yes / no

4. Do you think everyone feels lonely at some time in his or her life? Do you think this is common? Explain your answer.

5. Read the title of this chapter again. What's *your* answer to this question?

Reading

Read the passage carefully. Then complete the exercises that follow.

CD 1
TR 7

Loneliness: How can we overcome it?

1 Most people feel lonely sometimes, but it usually only lasts between a few minutes
2 and a few hours. This kind of loneliness is not serious. In fact, it is quite normal.
3 For some people, though, loneliness can last for years. Psychologists are studying
4 this complex phenomenon in an attempt to better understand long-term loneliness.
5 These researchers have already identified three different types of loneliness.
6 The first kind of loneliness is temporary. This is the most common type. It usually
7 disappears quickly and does not require any special attention. The second kind,
8 situational loneliness, is a natural result of a particular situation–for example, a divorce,
9 the death of a loved one, moving to a new place, or going away to college. Although this
10 kind of loneliness can cause physical problems, such as headaches and sleeplessness, it
11 usually does not last for more than a year. Situational loneliness is easy to understand
12 and to predict.
13 The third kind of loneliness is the most severe. Unlike the second type, chronic
14 loneliness usually lasts more than two years and has no specific cause. People who
15 experience habitual loneliness have problems socializing and becoming close to
16 others. Unfortunately, many chronically lonely people think there is little or nothing

they can do to improve their condition. Psychologists agree that one important factor in loneliness is a person's social contacts, e.g., friends, family members, coworkers, etc. We depend on various people for different reasons. For instance, our families give us emotional support, our parents and teachers give us guidance, and our friends share similar interests and activities. However, psychologists have found that the number of social contacts we have is not the only reason for loneliness. It is more important how many social contacts we think or expect we should have. In other words, though lonely people may have many social contacts, they sometimes feel they should have more. They question their own popularity.

Most researchers agree that the loneliest people are between the ages of 18 and 25, so a group of psychologists decided to study a group of college freshmen. They found that more than 50 percent of the freshmen were situationally lonely at the beginning of the semester as a result of their new circumstances, but adjusted after a few months. Thirteen percent were still lonely after seven months due to shyness and fear. They felt very uncomfortable meeting new people, even though they understood that their fear was not rational. The situationally lonely freshmen overcame their loneliness by making new friends, but the chronically lonely remained unhappy because they were afraid to do so.

Psychologists are trying to find ways to help habitually lonely people for two reasons. First of all, they are unhappy and unable to socialize. Secondly, researchers have found a connection between chronic loneliness and serious illnesses, such as heart disease. While temporary and situational loneliness can be a normal, healthy part of life, chronic loneliness can be a very sad, and sometimes dangerous, condition.

Fact Finding

Read the passage again. Then read the following statements. Check (√) whether each statement is True or False. If a statement is false, rewrite it so that it is true. Then go back to the passage and find the line that supports your answer.

1. _____ True __X__ False   Psychologists say there are two different kinds of loneliness.

   they sey 3 _____

2. _____ True __X__ False   All kinds of loneliness last only a short time.

   the Temporary is the onley is for short time

3. _____ True __X__ False   Temporary loneliness is very serious.

   Cronelley _____

4. __✓__ True _____ False   Divorce sometimes causes loneliness.

   _____

5. __✓__ True _____ False   Loneliness can cause sleeplessness and headaches.

   _____

6. __✓__ True _____ False   Chronic loneliness usually lasts more than two years.

   _____

7. _____ True __X__ False   Lonely people have no social contacts.

   _____

8. _____ True __X__ False   The loneliest people are over 50 years old.

   bet wen 18-25 _____

9. __✓__ True _____ False   Chronic loneliness can cause serious illness.

   _____

Reading Analysis

Read each question carefully. Circle the letter or the number of the correct answer, or write the answer in the space provided.

1. Read the first paragraph.

  a. **Lasts** means
1. finishes.
2. hurts.
3. continues.

  b. **Normal** means
1. serious.
2. usual.
3. unhappy.

  c. **Complex** means
1. simple.
2. difficult.
3. new.

  d. A **phenomenon** is
1. an occurrence.
2. a psychologist.
3. a mistake.

  e. **This complex phenomenon** refers to
1. loneliness that lasts for years.
2. loneliness that lasts for hours.

  f. **Long-term** means
1. normal.
2. serious.
3. continual.

  g. **Identified** means
1. named.
2. understood.
3. researched.

2. Read the second paragraph.

  a. Something **temporary**
1. lasts a short time.
2. is serious.
3. is very common.

  b. A **situation** refers to
1. a negative experience.
2. a positive experience.
3. an existing condition.

c. When we **predict** something, we
   1. recognize it before it happens.
   2. worry about it.
   3. know it is negative.

3. Read lines 13–15.
   a. What does **unlike** show?
      1. A similarity
      2. A difference
      3. An addition
   b. Which word in these lines is a synonym for **chronic**?

      Sure

4. Read lines 17–21.
   a. A **factor** is
      1. a problem that you have.
      2. a situation that you are in.
      3. a reason for something.
   b. What follows **e.g.**?
      1. Examples
      2. Proof
      3. Explanations
   c. **Etc.** means
      1. for example.
      2. and others.
      3. end of sentence.
   d. **For instance** introduces
      1. explanations.
      2. examples.
      3. results.
   e. **Guidance** means
      1. information.
      2. advice.
      3. contacts.

5. Read lines 22–25.
   a. How does **in other words** help you?
      1. It introduces additional information.
      2. It introduces a different idea.
      3. It introduces the same information in different words.
   b. **Question** means
      1. ask a question.
      2. are not sure.
      3. worry about.

6. Read lines 26–30.

   a. **Circumstances** refers to
      1. the loneliness you feel.
      2. the situation you are in.
      3. the college where you study.

   b. **Adjusted** means
      1. got used to the situation.
      2. made friends.
      3. felt uncomfortable.

7. Read lines 32–34.

   a. When you **overcome** something, you
      1. run away from it.
      2. are comfortable with it.
      3. change it to make it better.

   b. What does **the situationally lonely freshmen overcame their loneliness** mean?
      1. They accepted their loneliness.
      2. They were no longer lonely.
      3. They made new friends.

   c. **They were afraid to do so** means

   _____

8. Read lines 38–39. **While** means

   a. at the same time.
   b. during.
   c. although.

9. What is the main idea of the passage?

   a. There are three kinds of loneliness with different causes and effects.
   b. Chronic loneliness is the most severe kind of loneliness.
   c. Researchers want to cure all kinds of loneliness because they may be harmful.

Vocabulary Skills

PART 1

Recognizing Word Forms

In English, there are several ways that adjectives become nouns. Some adjectives become nouns by adding the suffix -ness, for example, sick (adj.), sickness (n.).

Complete each sentence with the correct word form on the left. All the nouns are singular.

happy *(adj.)*

happiness *(n.)*

ill *(adj.)*

illness *(n.)*

lonely *(adj.)*

loneliness *(n.)*

shy *(adj.)*

shyness *(n.)*

sleepless *(adj.)*

sleeplessness *(n.)*

1. Chronically lonely people are not ____adj____ because they are unable to socialize. They can increase their ____n.____ by making new friends.

2. Lonely people can become very ____adj____. Some kinds of loneliness can cause a serious ____n____, such as heart disease.

3. The college students overcame their ____n____ by going out more often with their friends. They didn't feel ____adj____ anymore.

4. Many of the college freshmen were lonely due to ____n.____ and fear. They were too ____adj____ to meet new people.

5. Lonely people may also have ____adj____ nights. This is because loneliness often causes ____n____.

adj –> discrite the People

PART 2

Recognizing Sentence Connectors

Sentence connectors, such as *although, in fact, unfortunately, first of all, secondly,* and *in other words*, connect ideas and help make them clearer.

Read each sentence. Complete each sentence with *although, in fact, unfortunately, first of all, secondly,* or *in other words*. Use each sentence connector only once.

1. One type of loneliness is not serious. _in fact_, it is quite normal.

2. Situational loneliness is a natural result of a particular situation. _Although_ this kind of loneliness can cause physical problems, it usually does not last for more than a year.

3. People who experience habitual loneliness have problems socializing. _unfortunately,_ they think there is little or nothing they can do to improve their condition.

4. Psychologists are trying to find ways to help habitually lonely people for two reasons.

   First of all, they are unhappy and unable to socialize. _Secondly_, researchers have found a connection between chronic loneliness and serious illnesses such as heart disease.

5. It is more important how many social contacts we think or expect we should have.

   In other words, lonely people feel they should have more social contacts.

Vocabulary in Context

Read the following sentences. Complete each sentence with the correct word or phrase from the box. Use each word or phrase only once.

adjusted *(v.)*	factor *(n.)*	~~stay~~ remain *(v.)*	~~short time~~ temporary *(adj.)*
~~on going~~ chronic *(adj.)*	for instance	~~friendly~~ shy *(adj.)*	unlike *(prep.)*
circumstances *(n.)*	overcame *(v.)*		

1. Helen is very thin, _un like_ her sister, who is quite heavy.

2. After Marco learns English, he will _remain_ in this country and get a good job.

3. This beautiful weather is only _temporary_. It is going to rain for the rest of this week.

4. Anna finally _overcome_ her fear of flying when she traveled to Florida by plane last month.

5. I am always waiting for Debbie because she is late for everything. Her _Chronic_ *(on going)* lateness is destroying our friendship.

6. Emily is a _shy_ student. She is very quiet and always sits alone in class.

7. Carlo went to a new university last semester. He _adjusted_ very well and has many new friends.

8. A proper diet is an important _factor_ in maintaining good health.

9. Barbara has many varied interests. _For instance_, she enjoys music, horseback riding, and coin collecting.

10. Many _circumstances_ contribute to situational loneliness. Going to a new school or moving to a new city are examples.

Reading Skill

Creating a Flowchart

Flowcharts show certain kinds of information, such as cause and effect, and how people come to conclusions. Creating a flowchart can help you organize and understand important information from a reading passage.

Read the passage on pages 83–84 again. Then complete the flowchart with information from the passage.

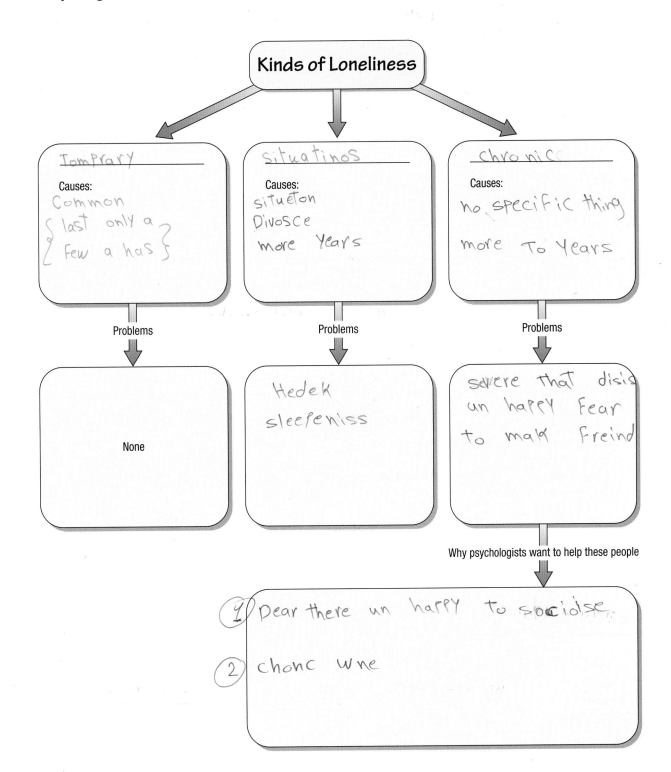

Kinds of Loneliness

Tomprary
Causes:
Common
last only a
few a has

Situatinos
Causes:
situeton
Divosce
more Years

Chronicc
Causes:
no specific thing
more To Years

Problems → None

Problems → Hedek
sleepeniss

Problems → severe that disis
un happy Fear
to make Freind

Why psychologists want to help these people

1. Dear there un happy to sociolse.
2. chonc wne

Information Recall

Read the passage again, and review the flowchart. Then answer the questions.

1. How are the three kinds of loneliness different from each other?

   _____

   _____

   _____

   _____

   _____

2. Why is chronic loneliness the most severe kind of loneliness?

   _____

   _____

   _____

   _____

   _____

3. How can loneliness be unhealthy?

   _____

   _____

   _____

   _____

   _____

Writing a Summary

A summary is a short paragraph that provides the most important information from a reading. It usually does not include details, just the main ideas. When you write a summary, it is important to use your own words, and not copy directly from the reading.

Write a brief summary of the passage. The entire summary should not be more than four sentences. Use your own words. Be sure to indent the first line.

_____

_____

_____

_____

_____

_____

Topics for Discussion and Writing

1. In this article, the author states that young adults (18 to 25 years old) are the loneliest people in the United States. Think about this statement. What do you think may be some reasons for this?

2. Do you think it is important for psychologists and researchers to study loneliness? Why or why not?

3. Write in your journal. Describe a time in your life when you felt lonely. What did you do to overcome your loneliness?

Critical Thinking

1. Many lonely people have a lot of social contacts, but they feel they should have more. Why do you think they feel this way? Explain your answer.

2. What is an obstacle you had to overcome in your life? Or, what is an obstacle you may have to overcome in your future? Talk about this obstacle with a partner. What are some ways to overcome this obstacle?

3. In the article, the author states that in the United States, the loneliest people are young adults (18 to 25 years old). Is this also true in your country? Does loneliness differ from culture to culture? Take a survey in your class. Ask your classmates who they think the loneliest people are in their cultures. Use the chart on page 95 to record your answers. Then write the results of the survey on the board. With your classmates, discuss what you think are the reasons for these results.

Country	Loneliest Age Group	Possible Reasons
United States	18–25	Many young people are in college and away from home.

Crossword Puzzle

Review the words in the box below. Then read the clues on the next page. Write the words in the correct spaces in the puzzle.

adjust	factor	normal	question
chronic	guidance	overcome	situation
circumstances	identify	phenomenon	temporary
complex	last	predict	unlike

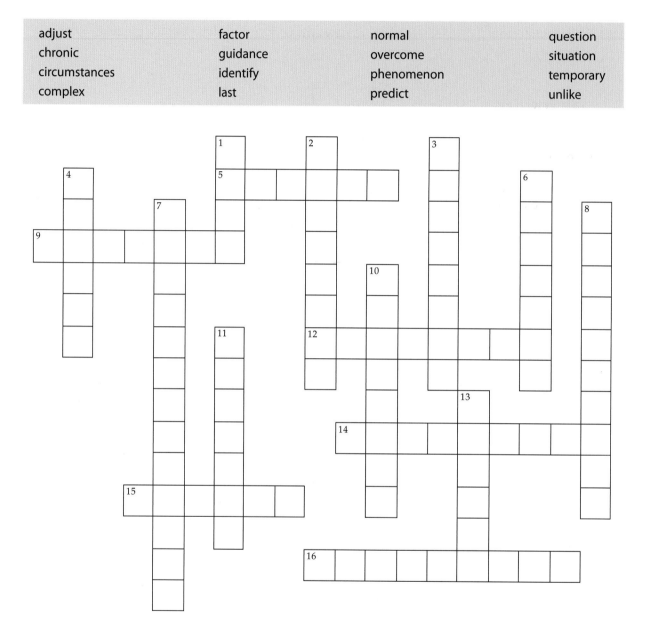

Crossword Puzzle Clues

ACROSS CLUES

5. People who can _____, or adapt, to new environments are less likely to become habitually lonely.

9. We can _____ some kinds of loneliness. For instance, we know we will probably be lonely in a new location.

12. Most people can _____ the two short-term kinds of loneliness, but the third kind of loneliness may last a very long time.

14. Some loneliness is caused by the _____ we are in, for example, a new school or city where we don't know anyone.

15. The first two types of loneliness are usually short-term, _____ the third type, which can continue for a very long time.

16. The second type of loneliness is _____. It is not permanent.

DOWN CLUES

1. If feelings of loneliness _____ for a long time, we need to get help to try to end it.

2. If you _____ how much other people like you, you may become very unhappy.

3. We depend on our family and teachers to give us _____ when we are not sure what to do.

4. Loneliness that continues for a few days is quite _____. Most people experience this.

6. People are very _____! Our personalities are not simple at all.

7. Some _____, such as unfamiliar people and places, can make us feel lonely.

8. Habitual loneliness is a _____ that needs special attention because it can become dangerous.

10. Can you _____ the three types of loneliness? What are they?

11. Another word for habitual loneliness is _____ loneliness.

13. An important _____ in loneliness is how many friends we believe we have.

Justice and Crime

Statue of Justice, Brussels, Belgium

1. According to the laws in the United States, "Justice is blind." What does this sentence mean?

2. Movies, TV shows, and books about crimes and criminals are very popular. Why do you think people are interested in these types of stories?

3. People often say that the punishment should fit the crime. What is the proper punishment for robbing a bank, for stealing a car, or for murder?

CHAPTER **7** Solving Crimes with Modern Technology

A forensic scientist dusting
a window for evidence

Prereading

1. Work in a small group. What types of technology can help solve crimes? Make a list in the chart below. When you are finished, share your list with the class.

Type of Technology	How can this help solve a crime?

2. Who are the different people that solve crimes? How are their jobs different from each other? How do they try to solve crimes?

Reading

Read the passage carefully. Then complete the exercises that follow.

Solving Crimes with Modern Technology

1   Solving crimes is one of the most important jobs of law enforcement. Improvements in
2 crime technology help investigators identify suspects and solve crimes faster and more
3 efficiently. Detectives even use this technology today to solve crimes from a long time ago.
4   A well-known example of new technology is DNA testing. Previously, when police
5 found body fluids such as blood, sweat, and saliva at a crime scene, they collected
6 it as evidence. However, this evidence could not be analyzed at that time. Even so,
7 crime experts stored it in a freezer. Today, modern DNA testing helps experts analyze
8 this type of evidence to solve recent crimes. They are reinvestigating "cold cases," too.
9 Cold cases are unsolved crimes from the past. Now criminologists have the modern
10 technology they require to analyze frozen evidence. In many cases, they identify
11 suspects with the information they get from it.
12   The murder of ten-year-old Anna Palmer is an example of a cold case. In 1998,
13 someone attacked and killed Anna outside her house in Salt Lake City, Utah. There
14 were no witnesses to the murder and very little evidence. Then in 2009, this cold case
15 was reopened. Experts examined dirt from under Anna's fingernails and found DNA
16 evidence. This DNA matched the DNA of Matthew Brock. In 2011, Brock pled guilty
17 to Anna's murder and is now in prison for life.
18   Another example of modern technology involves new kinds of fingerprint testing.
19 In the past, analysts could only examine fingerprint patterns and check them with the
20 ones they had on file. The fingerprints of convicted criminals are kept permanently
21 on file in police records. People whose fingerprints are not on file cannot be identified
22 in this way. Today, however, fingerprint testing provides additional information,
23 such as the age and sex of its owner. The fingerprints also reveal if the person takes
24 medication. Investigators can use this new technology to reanalyze fingerprints from
25 cold cases to help identify a suspect and even solve the crime.
26   In one case, the police in Tacoma, Washington, found the body of a 27-year-old
27 woman who had been murdered in her bedroom. There were no witnesses, and her
28 apartment had few clues. The only real evidence did not seem very helpful. The
29 victim's bed sheet had some of her blood on it and looked as if someone had wiped
30 his or her hands. At the time of the murder, it was impossible to identify a fingerprint,
31 or even a palm print, from fabric. The detectives could not use the evidence, but they
32 saved it. They called Eric Berg, a forensic expert with the Tacoma police, for help.
33 A forensic expert is a person who helps solve crimes.

Eric Berg is not only a forensic expert, but a computer expert, too. He developed computer software to enhance, or improve, crime scene photos. He used his software and reexamined the fabric from the murder case. It worked! Eric Berg used his software to make the palm print more apparent, or clear. Then he gave the new evidence to the detectives. The detectives checked the palm print with clear palm prints they had on file. They identified a man whose palm print matched a print on file and arrested him. The court eventually convicted him of the crime, and he is now in jail. Today, many other police departments have reopened old cases and are using Eric Berg's software.

Police are developing other kinds of new crime-solving technology that are enabling them to reconsider evidence they could not use in the past. By helping the police identify suspects, new technology may help solve cold cases as well as current cases and put more criminals in prison.

A forensic scientist securing a fingerprint

Fact Finding

Read the passage again. Then read the following statements. Check (√) whether each statement is True or False. If a statement is false, rewrite it so that it is true. Then go back to the passage and find the line that supports your answer.

1. _____ True _____ False̶ Fingerprint testing always helps to solve crimes.

_____

2. _____ True _____ False Modern fingerprint technology can identify body fluids.

_____

3. _____ True̶ _____ False When a woman was murdered in Tacoma, Washington, it was impossible to identify a fingerprint from fabric.

_____

4. _____ True _____ False Eric Berg developed new software to improve photos.

_____

5. _____ True _____ False Eric Berg's technology may help solve older crimes, too.

_____

6. _____ True _____ False In the past, detectives never took samples of evidence at a crime scene.

_____

7. _____ True _____ False Detectives can always solve cold cases with new technology.

_____

Reading Analysis

Read each question carefully. Circle the letter or the number of the correct answer, or write your answer in the space provided.

1. Read lines 1–3. **Law enforcement** means
   a. making sure people obey the law.
   b. writing laws to solve crimes.
   c. creating new technology.

2. Read lines 4–8.

a. **Previously** means
   1. unfortunately.
   2. in the past. ☑
   3. surprisingly.

b. What are **blood**, **sweat**, and **saliva**?

   evidnce

c. How do you know?

   becouse they collet thet to want him Found that.

d. A crime **scene** is
   1. the place where the crime occurred. ☑
   2. the evidence of a crime.
   3. a collection of body fluids.

e. In the past, what did the police sometimes do with evidence they could not identify?
   1. They threw it away.
   2. They didn't collect it.
   3. They saved it. ☑

f. **Analyze** means
   1. inspect carefully. ☑
   2. collect.
   3. store.

3. Read line 9. **Cold cases** are

a. crimes that were committed in the winter.
b. old crimes that have not been solved. ☑
c. recent cases that are unsolvable.

4. Read lines 15–16. **This DNA matched the DNA of Matthew Brock.**

a. This sentence means
   1. the DNA was Matthew Brock's. ☑
   2. the DNA was the only evidence of the crime.
   3. the DNA was different from Matthew Brock's DNA.

b. **Matched** means
   1. was different from.
   2. was the same as. ☑
   3. was similar to.

5. Read lines 20–21. Whose prints are already on file?

a. People who have never committed a crime in the past
b. People who have been convicted of a crime in the past ☑
c. All the people who live in a city, state, or country

6. Read lines 27–30.

   a. Which word is a synonym for **clues**?

   _____

   b. A **victim** is

      1. the person who commits a crime.

      ☑ 2. the person who is harmed by a crime.

7. Read lines 30–33.

   a. What is a type of **fabric**?

      ① A bed sheet

      2. A fingerprint

      3. Blood

   b. What was the only evidence the Tacoma police had?

   _____

   c. An **expert** is a person who

      1. is very skilled at working with evidence.

      2. is very skilled at working with computers.

      ③ is very skilled at working in a special field.

   d. What is a **forensic expert**?

   _____

8. Read lines 34–37.

   a. **Software** refers to

      1. computers.

      ☑ 2. computer programs.

      3. photos.

   b. **Enhance** means _To improve to or make it better._ .

   c. How do you know?

   _____

   d. A synonym for **apparent** is

      1. new.

      ☑ 2. clear.

      3. evidence.

9. Read lines 42–43.

   a. **Enabling** means

      ① allowing.

      2. making.

      3. telling.

b. **Reconsider** means
1. solve quickly.
2. think over again.
3. get rid of.

10. What is the main idea of the passage?
a. New technology always solves every crime, even old ones.
b. New technology helps solve many crimes, even old ones.
c. New technology is only useful in solving murders.

Vocabulary Skills

PART 1

Recognizing Word Forms

In English, there are several ways that verbs change to nouns. Some verbs become nouns by adding the suffix -*ment*, for example, *arrange (v.), arrangement (n.)*.

Complete each sentence with the correct word form on the left. Use the correct form of the verb. The nouns may be singular or plural.

improve *(v.)*

improvement *(n.)*

1. Criminologists have made many _____ in the ways they now solve crimes. New technology _____ the ability of the police to catch criminals.

enhance *(v.)*

enhancement *(n.)*

2. Eric Berg's software _____ crime scene photos. Criminologists use these _____ to identify evidence.

enforce *(v.)*

enforcement *(n.)*

3. One of a police officer's jobs is law _____. A police officer not only _____ the law, but also tries to help prevent crimes from happening.

develop *(v.)*

development *(n.)*

4. Eric Berg _____ computer software to help solve crimes. The _____ of new software programs is helpful to forensic experts.

require *(v.)*

requirement *(n.)*

5. Forensic experts sometimes _____ modern technology to identify suspects in a crime. However, this _____ is not always necessary when there are several witnesses to the crime.

PART 2

The Prefix *re-*

In English, the prefix *re-* means *again*. It can be added to many words, especially verbs; for example, *rewrite* means *write again* when the prefix *re-* is added to *write*.

Read the following sentences. Complete each sentence with the correct word from the box. Use each word only once.

⑤ reanalyze *mean: study*	③ reexamine *mean: look at...*
④ reconsider *mean: think about...*	② reinvestigate *mean: get information, look*
	① reopen *mean: start, or look for answer*

1. Unsolved murder cases are never really closed. The police will ___reopen___ a case

   and try to find the murderer if new evidence becomes available.

2. The police have started to ___reinvestigate___ a 20-year-old murder case. They think they

   can solve it now.

3. Improved fingerprint testing enables experts to ___reexamine___ fingerprints for more

   information, such as the age and sex of the owner.

4. Investigators are going to ___reconsider___ opening several old unsolved cases. However,

   they are not sure they have enough evidence.

5. In the past, investigators could get only a little information from blood, such as blood

   type. Now they can ___reanalyze___ blood for much more information that will help

   them identify a crime suspect.

Vocabulary in Context

Read the following sentences. Complete each sentence with the correct word or phrase from the box. Use each word or phrase only once.

arrest *(v.)*	criminologists *(n.)*	pattern *(n.)*
clues *(n.)*	enforce *(v.)*	reopen *(v.)*
convict *(v.)*	evidence *(n.)*	scene *(n.)*

1. Police officers, detectives, and many other people _enforce_ the law in a variety of ways.

2. Much _evidence_ is required in order to identify a suspect and solve a crime.

3. Today, investigators frequently _reopen_ cold cases because they can reexamine stored evidence for new information.

4. _clues_, such as hair and skin, provide very good evidence for identifying crime suspects.

5. Sometimes police can match the _pattern_ of a car tire from a crime scene with a design from the tire manufacturer.

6. Only police investigators are permitted at the _scene_ of a crime.

7. Courts cannot _convict_ a person without sufficient evidence to prove the person is guilty.

8. _Criminologists_ are very skilled at solving crimes.

9. The police can only _arrest_ someone when they have enough evidence to suspect that person of having committed a crime.

Reading Skill

Understanding Line Graphs

Line graphs often contain important information. It's important to understand them. Line graphs compare numbers or amounts, and give you information about the reading.

Read the line graphs. Then answer the questions.

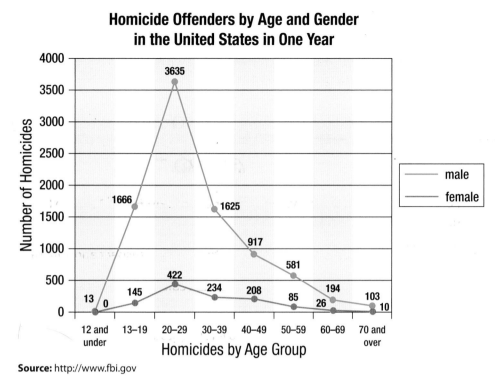

Homicide Offenders by Age and Gender in the United States in One Year

Source: http://www.fbi.gov

1. Who is an offender?

   a. The victim

   (b.) The killer

2. What gender and age group committed the most murders in this one-year period?

   a. Males between 13 and 19

   b. Females between 13 and 19

   (c.) Males between 20 and 29

   d. Females between 20 and 29

3. What gender and age group committed the fewest murders in this one-year period?

   a. Males under 12

   (b.) Females under 12

   c. Males over 70

   d. Females over 70

4. What can we conclude from this graph? Check (√) all that apply.

   _X_ a. As people get older, they are more likely to commit homicide.

   _✓_ b. At any age, more males than females commit homicide.

   _✓_ c. The very young and those over 70 are the least likely to commit homicide.

   _X_ d. Females and males are equally likely to commit homicide.

   _✓_ e. Males between 20 and 29 years of age commit more murders than females of all ages combined.

   _✓_ f. Even children commit murder.

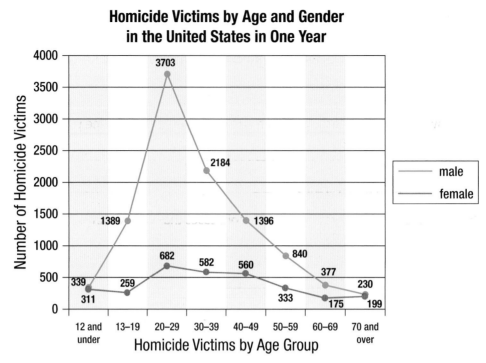

**Homicide Victims by Age and Gender
in the United States in One Year**

Number of Homicide Victims

3703

2184

1389   1396

840

682   582   560   377

339   259   230
311   333   175   199

male
female

12 and   13–19   20–29   30–39   40–49   50–59   60–69   70 and
under   over

Homicide Victims by Age Group

Source: https://www.census.gov/compendia/statab/2012/tables/12s0311.pdf

1. Who is a homicide victim?
   a. The person who is killed
   b. The killer

2. Who is least likely to be a victim of a murder?
   a. A male aged 70 or older
   b. A female under 12 years of age
   c. A female between 60 and 69 years old

3. What can we conclude from this graph? Check (√) all that apply.
   ____✗____ a. Children under 12 are the least likely to be murdered.
   ____✓____ b. Older people are the least likely to be murdered.
   ____✓____ c. More males between 20 and 29 years old are murdered than any other group.
   ____✓____ d. The very young and those over 70 are the least likely to be murdered.
   ____✗____ e. At any age, more females than males are murdered.
   ____✓____ f. More males between 20 and 29 years of age are murdered than all females of
         every age combined.

Information Recall

Read the passage again, and review the information in the line graphs. Then answer the questions.

1. How is fingerprint testing today more helpful than it was in the past?

   _____

   _____

2. How are investigators able to solve cold cases that were unsolvable in the past?

   _____

   _____

3. Who is most likely to be both a homicide offender and a homicide victim?

   _____

   _____

Writing a Summary

A summary is a short paragraph that provides the most important information from a reading. It usually does not include details, just the main ideas. When you write a summary, it is important to use your own words, and not copy directly from the reading.

Write a brief summary of the passage. The summary should not be more than four sentences. Use your own words. Be sure to indent the first line.

_____

_____

_____

_____

_____

Topics for Discussion and Writing

1. In the United States, the fingerprints of convicted criminals are kept on file permanently. Do you agree with this policy? Or do you think the fingerprints should not be on file after the criminal comes out of jail? Why? Explain your opinion.

2. Criminal investigators try to collect as much evidence as they can in order to identify the person who committed a crime. How much evidence does a jury need in order to convict a person of a crime?

3. Many people's fingerprints are not on file. As a result, fingerprints from a crime scene may not help criminal investigators find the criminal. Should the law require all people to put their fingerprints on file even if they have never committed a crime? Explain your reasons for your answer.

4. Look at the DNA samples below.
   a. Which suspect's DNA is the best match for the DNA sample found at a crime scene?
   b. Does this DNA match prove that this suspect committed the crime? Why or why not?

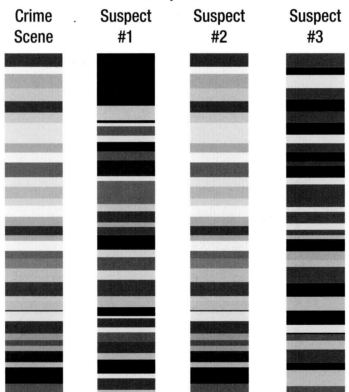

DNA Samples From:

Crime Scene   Suspect #1   Suspect #2   Suspect #3

Source: http://evolution.berkeley.edu/evolibrary/news/060301_crime

5. Write in your journal. Chapter 7 discusses some new kinds of technology to help solve crimes. Which new technology do you think is the most important one? Why? What types of crimes do you think it can help solve?

Critical Thinking

1. Each person's fingerprints are unique and do not change over the person's lifetime. Scientists studied fingerprint patterns and developed a system for classifying them by type in order to make identification more accurate. Examine the sample fingerprints below.

Figure 1: Arch

Figure 2: Left loop

Figure 3: Right loop

Figure 4: Tent

Figure 5: Whorl

Source: National Institute of Standards and Technology

On a separate sheet of paper, using an ink pad, make your own fingerprint and compare it to the samples. Which pattern does your fingerprint have? How is it similar to that pattern? What are the differences that make it clear they are not the same fingerprint? When you have finished, be sure to destroy the paper with your fingerprint on it.

2. Go online to a search engine such as Google to find a website with sample fingerprints and fingerprint-matching games. Use these key words: "classifying fingerprints" or "fingerprint samples and how to classify them." Examine the sample prints. Then do a fingerprint-matching game. See if you can identify the print taken from a crime scene.

3. Eric Berg used his own time and money to improve crime scene photos. Why do you think he worked so hard at this? What might be some reasons? Compare your answers with those of your classmates.

Crossword Puzzle

Review the words in the box below. Then read the clues on the next page. Write the words in the correct spaces in the puzzle.

6 analyze
apparent
7 blood
17 clues
2 enable

8 enforcement
9 enhance
experts
12 fabric

5 forensic
11 match
13 and 3 pattern
16 previously

14 reconsider
15 scene
1 technology
4 unsolved

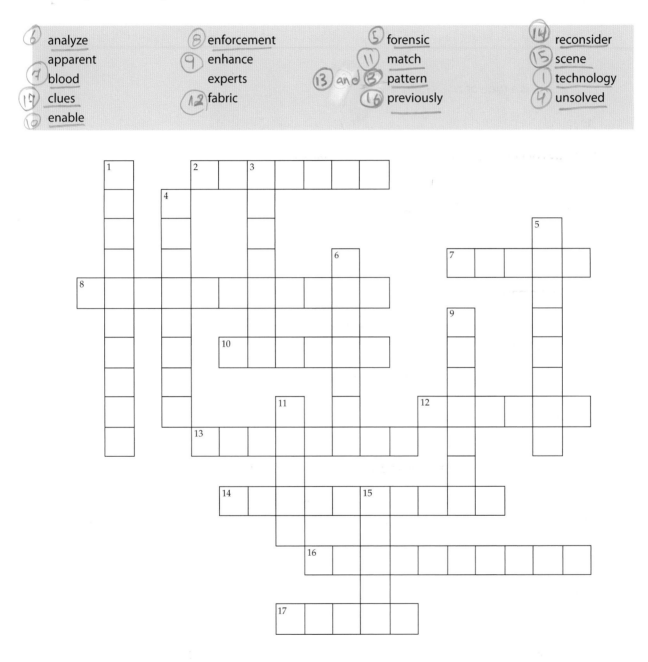

Crossword Puzzle Clues

ACROSS CLUES

2. Many _experts_ _____ help the police solve crimes. Some work with computers; others work with photography, for example.

7. _Blood_ _____ is a type of body fluid.

8. The job of the police is law _____. They try to make sure that laws are obeyed.

10. New ways of crime solving _____ investigators to solve many crimes.

12. Sometimes a piece of _____, such as material from a coat, becomes important evidence in a crime.

13. The man's guilt was _____, or clear, from the evidence, so the man pled guilty to the murder.

14. Investigators often _____ old murder cases because they can use evidence that was not useful in the past.

16. _____, police could only look at the design of fingerprints. Today, they can get much more information from fingerprints.

17. _Clues_ _____ are evidence that police find and collect at the scene of a crime.

DOWN CLUES

1. Modern _____, such as powerful computers and improved photography, help police identify suspects.

3. The _____ of every person's fingerprints is unique. No one has exactly the same fingerprints.

4. There are many _____ crimes that investigators hope to find answers to one day.

5. Eric Berg often provides useful _____ evidence to police after he studies it.

6. Experts carefully _____ fingerprints, body fluids, material, and other evidence from every crime.

9. Some computer programs can _____ an image so it can be used as evidence in a crime case.

11. Every person's DNA is unique. When police find a _____ between a suspect and DNA from a crime scene, they are confident that the person may be guilty.

15. The _____ of a crime is the place where the crime took place.

Women in a police lineup

Prereading

1. What kinds of evidence are used to convict suspected criminals? In small groups, use the chart below to make a list of the kinds of evidence used to convict criminals for each crime.

Crime	Murder	Bank Robbery	Mugging
Types of Evidence			

2. In your country, what kinds of evidence are used to convict criminals for these crimes?

3. Look at the photo on page 116. Where was this photo taken? Who are the four women? Why are they there?

4. In your country, is an eyewitness's testimony important in convicting criminals?

5. In your opinion, what kinds of people make reliable eyewitnesses? Why?

Reading

🎧 **Read the passage carefully. Then complete the exercises that follow.**
CD 1
TR 9

The Reliability of Eyewitnesses

1   One night, when Jennifer Thompson was a 22-year-old college student, someone
2 broke into her apartment and attacked her. During the attack, Jennifer tried to observe
3 and remember details about the man who raped her. The next day, she identified
4 her attacker in a lineup. When the case went to court, she positively identified
5 Ronald Cotton as the man who raped her that night. The court believed the victim's
6 testimony, convicted Ronald Cotton, and sentenced him to life in prison. But Jennifer
7 Thompson was wrong. Eleven years after she first identified Ronald Cotton as
8 her attacker, Ronald provided a blood sample for a DNA test.[1] Then the DNA was
9 compared to evidence from the attack. When Jennifer received the results of the DNA
10 test, she was shocked. Her attacker was not Ronald Cotton! Instead, her attacker was
11 a man named Bobby Poole. The two men were similar in appearance. Ronald Cotton
12 had spent 11 years in prison for a crime he did not commit. Bobby Poole confessed to
13 the crime. He was sentenced to prison, where he died several years later.

14   The jury convicted Ronald Cotton because of the eyewitness's testimony. They
15 believed Jennifer Thompson. She positively identified Cotton as the man who
16 attacked her. As a result, Ronald Cotton lost 11 years of his life. Jennifer Thompson
17 saw the man who attacked her, yet she mistakenly identified an innocent person.
18 Similar incidents have occurred before. Eyewitnesses to other crimes have identified
19 the wrong person in a police lineup or in photos.

20   Many factors influence the accuracy of eyewitness testimony. For instance, witnesses
21 sometimes see photos of several suspects before they try to identify the person they
22 saw in a lineup of people. They can become confused by seeing many photos of similar
23 faces. The number of people in the lineup and whether it is a live lineup or a photo may
24 also affect a witness's decision. People sometimes have difficulty identifying people of
25 other races. The questions the police ask witnesses also have an effect on them.

---

[1]DNA testing was not available at the time when Jennifer Thompson was attacked.

Are some witnesses more reliable than others? Many people believe that police officers are more reliable than ordinary people because they are experienced. Psychologists decided to test this idea. Two psychologists showed a film of crimes to both police officers and civilians. Their findings were conclusive. The psychologists found no difference between the police and the civilians in correctly remembering the details of the crimes.

Sometimes the testimony of several eyewitnesses may be inconsistent. They may remember details differently. However, despite all the possibilities for inaccuracy, courts cannot exclude eyewitness testimony from a trial. American courts depend on eyewitness testimony to resolve court cases. Frequently, it is the only evidence to a crime such as rape. Furthermore, eyewitness testimony is often correct. Although people do sometimes make mistakes, many times they really do identify individuals correctly.

American courts depend on the ability of the 12 jurors—not the judges—to determine the accuracy of the witness's testimony. It is their responsibility to decide if a certain witness could actually see, hear, and remember what occurred. In a few cases, the testimony of eyewitnesses has convicted innocent people. However, it has frequently resulted in the conviction of guilty people. Consequently, eyewitness testimony continues to be of great value in the American judicial system.

Fact Finding

Read the passage again. Then read the following statements. Check (√) whether each statement is True or False. If a statement is false, rewrite it so that it is true. Then go back to the passage and find the line that supports your answer.

1. _____ True _√_ False   Ronald Cotton went to jail for 11 years because he was guilty.

    Ronald Cotton was not guilty

2. _√_ True _____ False   Jennifer Thompson was sure Cotton attacked her, but she was wrong.

    _____ was wrong, her attacker was a man named Bobby Poole.

3. _√_ True _____ False   DNA testing proved that Ronald Cotton was innocent.

    _____

4. _√_ True _____ False   Some witnesses become confused when they see too many
                            photos of similar people.

    _____

5. _____ True _√_ False   Police officers are better witnesses than ordinary people.

    _no differences between the police and the civilians
    in correctly remembering the details of the crimes._

6. _√_ True _____ False   American courts depend a lot on eyewitness testimony.

    _____

7. _____ True _√_ False   The judge must decide if a witness's story is accurate.

    _The courts depend on the ability of the 12 jurors
    not the judges._

Reading Analysis

Read each question carefully. Circle or check (√) the letter or the number of the correct answer, or write the answer in the space provided.

1. According to the passage, which of the following factors influence eyewitnesses? Check (√)
    the correct ones.

    _√_ a. Seeing many similar photos

    _____ b. The time of day the crime happened

    _√_ c. The questions the police ask

_____ d. The age and sex of the witness

✓ e. Seeing a live lineup or a photo of a group of people

_____ f. The type of job the witness has

_____ g. The education of the witness

✓ h. The race of the suspect

2. Read lines 3–6.

a. **Identified** means

   1. spoke to.

   ②. recognized.

   3. photographed.

b. A **lineup** is

   ①. a group of people presented to a witness by the police.

   2. a long line of people who are photographed.

   3. a list of people who have committed crimes.

c. Who does the **victim** refer to?

   1. The person who commits a crime

   ②. The person a crime is committed against

d. What does **testimony** mean?

   ①. A person's statement used for evidence

   2. A photo used for evidence

   3. A clue used for evidence

3. Read lines 9–13.

a. She was **shocked** means she

   1. did not believe the results.

   ②. was surprised and upset.

   3. was happy about the results.

b. **Instead** means

   ①. rather.

   2. additionally.

   3. surprisingly.

c. **Bobby Poole confessed to the crime.** This sentence means

   1. Poole said he did not commit the crime.

   2. Poole said that Cotton committed the crime.

   ③. Poole admitted he committed the crime.

d. The two men were similar in **appearance**. **Appearance** means the two men

   1. committed similar crimes.

   ②. were similar in how they looked.

   3. were similar in how they worked.

4. Read lines 14–19.

    a. An **eyewitness** is a person who

        1. spoke to someone who saw a crime being committed.

        2. heard about a crime being committed.

        3. actually saw a crime being committed.

    b. What does **yet** mean?

        1. After

        2. So

        3. But

    c. An **incident** is

        1. an event.

        2. a crime.

        3. a kind of evidence.

5. Read lines 20–22.

    a. What does **accuracy** mean?

        1. Mistake

        2. Factor

        3. Correctness

    b. What does **for instance** mean?

        1. In addition

        2. For example

        3. However

6. In line 26, **reliable** means

    a. careful.

    b. nervous.

    c. dependable.

7. Read lines 28–31.

    a. Who are **civilians**?

        1. Police officers

        2. Ordinary people

        3. Psychologists

    b. What does **conclusive** mean?

        1. Certain

        2. Doubtful

        3. Shocking

8. Read lines 32–35.

    a. Testimony that is **inconsistent** is

        1. similar.

        2. false.

        3. different.

b. What does **despite** mean?
1. In addition to
2. As a result
3. In spite of

c. What does **resolve** mean?
1. Settle
2. Hear
3. Learn

9. Read lines 38–40: **"It is their responsibility to decide if . . ."** Who does **their** refer to?
a. The judges
b. The courts
c. The jurors

10. Read lines 40–43. What does **consequently** mean?
a. As a result
b. However
c. In addition

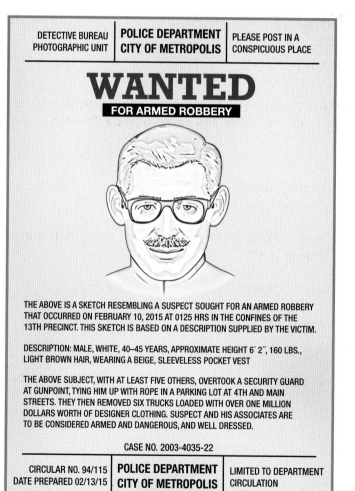

11. Refer to the wanted poster on the previous page. In small groups, answer the following questions.
   a. Who is this man? *Their*
   b. Who drew this picture?
   c. What do the police think this man did?
   d. Where can you see wanted posters?

12. What is the main idea of the passage?
   a. Ronald Cotton spent 11 years in jail, but he was innocent.
   b. Eyewitness testimony, although sometimes incorrect, is valuable.
   c. Police officers are not better eyewitnesses than civilians.

Vocabulary Skills

PART 1

Recognizing Word Forms

In English, there are several ways that verbs change to nouns. Some verbs become nouns by adding the suffix *-ence* or *-ance*, for example, *insist (v.), insistence (n.); resemble (v.), resemblance (n.)*.

Complete each sentence with the correct word form on the left. Use the correct form of the verb in either the affirmative or the negative. The nouns may be singular or plural.

depend *(v.)*

dependence *(n.)*

1. The court _____ (v) _____ on the ability of the 12 jurors to determine the accuracy of testimony. This _____ (n) _____ is an important part of the American court system.

differ *(v.)*

difference *(n.)*

2. The psychologists found no _____ (n) _____ between the police and the civilians in correctly remembering the details of the crimes. In other words, the two groups _____ (v) _____ in their ability.

occur *(v.)*

occurrence *(n.)*

3. When the crime _____ (v) _____, Jennifer Thompson mistakenly identified an innocent person. Unfortunately, this is not an unusual _____ (n) _____.

assist *(v.)*

assistance *(n.)*

4. Eyewitnesses _____ (v) _____ the police in solving crimes. Detectives often depend on this _____ (n) _____ to help them find criminals.

appear *(v.)*

appearance *(n.)*

5. Ronald Cotton and Bobby Poole had similar _____ (n) _____. The victim made a mistake because the two men _____ (v) _____ similar.

PART 2

The Prefix _in-_

In English, the prefix _in-_ means _not_. It can be added to many words, especially adjectives, for example, _insincere_ means _not sincere_ when the prefix _in-_ is added to _sincere_.

Read the following sentences. Complete each sentence with the correct word from the box. Use each word only once.

4 inconclusive	1 incorrect	3 infrequent
2 inconsistent	5 inexperienced	

1. Jennifer Thompson was _incorrect_ when she identified Ronald Cotton as her attacker.

2. Sometimes eyewitnesses are _incosistent_ in their description of a suspect. One person may say the suspect had dark hair, and another may say the suspect had light hair.

3. Juries hope that mistakes in eyewitness testimony are _infrequent_, but they can actually occur often.

4. The fingerprint identification was _inconclusive_ because the fingerprints were not clear. However, the DNA identification was absolutely conclusive.

5. Civilians are often _inexperienced_ witnesses, but they can be just as reliable as police officers in correctly remembering details of a crime.

Vocabulary in Context

Read the following sentences. Complete each sentence with the correct word from the box. Use each word only once.

2 civilian (n.)	3 guilty (adj.)	6 reliable (adj.)	4 testimony (n.)
8 despite (prep.)	7 innocent (adj.)	9 similar (adj.)	1 victims (n.)
5 evidence (n.)	10 mistake (n.)		

1. Last week, an armed robber shot two men when he robbed City Bank. Afterwards, an ambulance took the two _victims_ to the hospital.

2. John was in the army for two years. At the end of his military service, he was happy to become a _civilian_ again.

3. Tommy stole a car, but the police caught and arrested him. Because Tommy was
   _guilty_____, he went to prison for six months.

4. Kathy saw the two men who robbed the supermarket. As a result of her _testimony_ in
   court, the two men were convicted and put into prison.

5. When the police investigate a crime, they look for _evidence_ such as fingerprints,
   footprints, hair, and clothing.

6. The buses in this city are very _reliable____. They always arrive on time and are never late.

7. Many people believed that Ronald had murdered his wife, but he was _innocent_.

8. _despite_____ the cold weather, Kay went to work without her coat.

9. Chris and his brother look very _similar____. They are both tall and thin, and both have
   light hair and blue eyes.

10. The waitress made a _mistake__. She gave me coffee, but I ordered tea.

Reading Skill

Using Headings to Create an Outline

Readings often have headings. Headings introduce new ideas or topics. They also introduce
details. Using headings to make an outline can help you understand and remember the most
important information from the reading.

**Read the passage again. Underline what you think are the main ideas. Then complete the
following outline, using the sentences that you have underlined to help you. You will use this
outline later to answer questions about the reading.**

    I. Ronald Cotton's Case

        A. His Crime: _____

        B. The Evidence: _____

        C. Reason for His Conviction: _____

        D. The Problem: _____

II. Factors Influencing the Accuracy of Eyewitness Testimony

    A. _____

    B. _____

    C. _____

    D. _____

    E. _____

III. Experiment to Test the Reliability of Police Officers and Ordinary People as Witnesses

    A. Experiment: _____

    B. Results: _____

IV. Why Courts Cannot Exclude Eyewitness Testimony from a Trial

    A. _____

    B. _____

Information Recall

Read the passage again, and review the outline. Answer the questions.

1. Why did Ronald Cotton go to prison?

_____

_____

2. Why did Jennifer Thompson believe that Cotton attacked her?

_____

_____

3. Why is eyewitness testimony important in an American court?

_____

_____

Writing a Summary

A summary is a short paragraph that provides the most important information from a reading. It usually does not include details, just the main ideas. When you write a summary, it is important to use your own words, and not copy directly from the reading.

Write a brief summary of the passage. The summary should not be more than four sentences. Use your own words. Be sure to indent the first line.

_____

_____

_____

_____

_____

Topics for Discussion and Writing

1. Ronald Cotton went to prison because Jennifer Thompson made a mistake in identity. Do you know about a similar case? Describe the case. If not, go online and find information about a case of mistaken identity. Tell your classmates about this case.

2. Police officers are not better eyewitnesses than ordinary people. What type of person do you think would be a very reliable eyewitness? Why? Discuss this with a partner.

3. Write in your journal. Have you ever witnessed a crime or an accident? Were you able to remember the exact details? Why or why not? Describe what happened.

Police officers investigating the scene of a fatal accident, Irvine, California

CHAPTER 9 Innocent until Proven Guilty: The Criminal Court System

A witness being sworn in before a judge in a courtroom

Prereading

1. In groups of three or four, discuss the job of the police. What do you think their responsibilities should be? What should they have the authority to do?

2. Read the title of this chapter. In the American legal system, a person accused of a crime is considered to be innocent until he or she is proven guilty in a court. In your country, does an accused person have to prove his or her innocence, or does the court have to prove the person's guilt?

3. Refer to the photo on pages 98–99. The woman represents justice. Why is she blindfolded? What do the scales in her left hand symbolize? What does the sword in her right hand symbolize?

Write a brief summary of the passage. The summary should not be more than four sentences. Use your own words. Be sure to indent the first line.

Topics for Discussion and Writing

1. Ronald Cotton went to prison because Jennifer Thompson made a mistake in identity. Do you know about a similar case? Describe the case. If not, go online and find information about a case of mistaken identity. Tell your classmates about this case.

2. Police officers are not better eyewitnesses than ordinary people. What type of person do you think would be a very reliable eyewitness? Why? Discuss this with a partner.

3. Write in your journal. Have you ever witnessed a crime or an accident? Were you able to remember the exact details? Why or why not? Describe what happened.

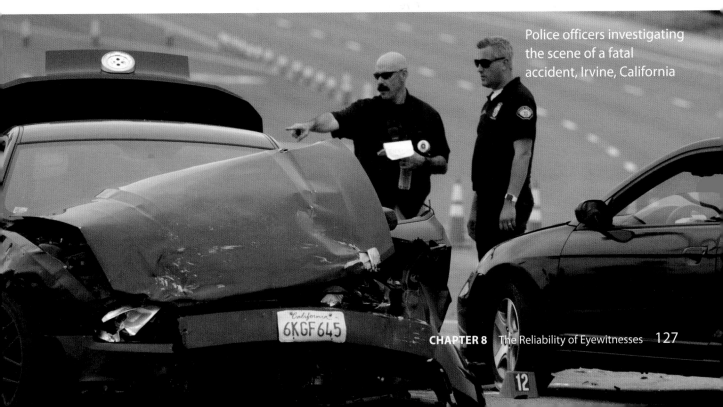

Police officers investigating the scene of a fatal accident, Irvine, California

Critical Thinking

1. What can the police do differently to help avoid cases of mistaken identity? With a partner, read the following sets of questions. Decide which one in each pair is the better question for the police to ask, and put a check (√) next to it. Compare your choices with your classmates' choices. Be prepared to explain your decisions.

   a. _____ 1. What was the suspect wearing?

      _____ 2. Was the suspect wearing a shirt and pants, or a suit?

   b. _____ 1. Did the suspect have a gun or a knife?

      _____ 2. Did the suspect have a weapon? If so, what did you see?

   c. _____ 1. Exactly what did the suspect look like? Describe the suspect's face in detail.

      _____ 2. Will you look at these photos and tell us which one is a photo of the suspect?

   d. _____ 1. What do you estimate was the suspect's height and weight?

      _____ 2. How tall and heavy was the suspect?

2. Eyewitness testimony is often unreliable. However, it continues to be part of the American legal system. Should eyewitness testimony be eliminated? Why or why not?

3. In this article, the victim made a mistake in identity. There are many factors that can cause people to make an error. Refer to the chart below. Work in small groups with your classmates. Which factors might confuse people and cause them to make mistakes in identity? Why? In the chart below, rank the factors in order of importance. Then write your reasons. For example, if you think that **weather** is the factor that would confuse people the most, write **1** next to **weather** under **Rank**.

Factor	Rank	Reason
sex (of witness/ of suspect)		
race (of witness/ of suspect)		

(continued)

Factor	Rank	Reason
age (of witness/ of suspect)		
time of day		
weather		
distance of witness from the crime		
level of education of the witness		

Crossword Puzzle

Review the words in the box below. Then read the clues on the next page. Write the words in the correct spaces in the puzzle.

accuracy	consequently	inconsistent	shocked
appearance	despite	lineup	testimony
civilians	eyewitness	reliable	victim
conclusive	identify	resolved	yet
confessed	incident		

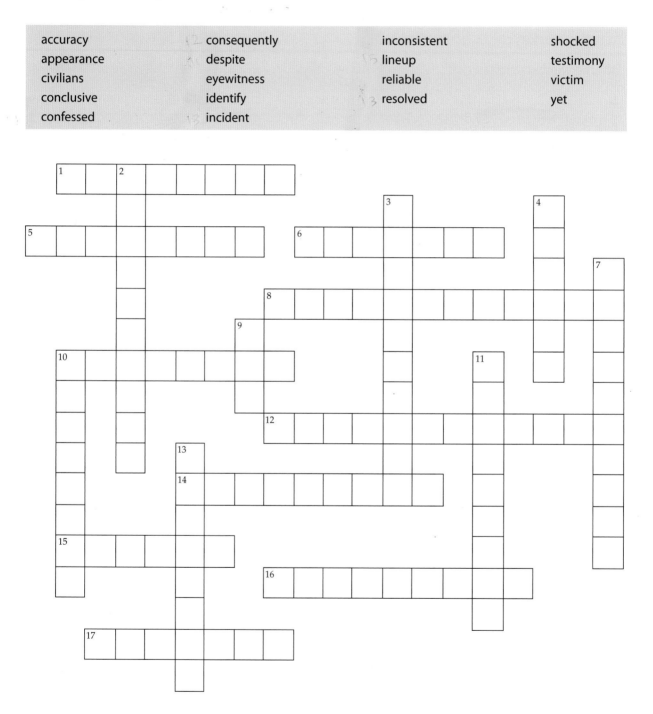

Crossword Puzzle Clues

ACROSS CLUES

1. A murder was committed at a bank. The _____ was reported in all the local newspapers.

5. The witness could not _____ the suspect because the crime occurred on a dark, rainy night.

6. _____ the fact that the murder weapon was never found, the man was convicted. There was other, very strong evidence against him.

8. I saw the crime being committed. _____, I reported it to the police.

10. Last year, the police _____ to find a better way to show suspects to witnesses. The old way wasn't working well.

12. The reports of the two witnesses are _____. One said the suspect was tall and thin. The other said the suspect was medium height and heavy.

14. When the suspect heard that five people saw him steal the car, he _____ to the crime.

15. The witness pointed out the suspect in a _____ at the police station.

16. Research shows that police officers are not more correct than _____ in describing a crime.

17. We were all _____ by the murder of our neighbor. It was a horrible crime.

DOWN CLUES

2. The evidence against the suspect was _____: three people saw her commit the crime, her fingerprints were on the weapon, and a security camera recorded her shooting the murdered man.

3. The _____ of the two suspects is very similar. We need additional evidence, such as fingerprints from the crime scene.

4. The young woman was the _____ of a robbery at night near her home.

7. A(n) _____ is a person who actually saw a crime being committed.

9. We were at the bank when three people robbed it, _____ we couldn't describe them because they had covered their faces.

10. Some people are more _____, or dependable, than others.

11. Witnesses who give _____ in court must promise to tell the truth.

13. I'm not sure about the _____ of this person's description of the suspect. Another person described the suspect differently.

A witness being sworn in before a judge in a courtroom

Prereading

1. In groups of three or four, discuss the job of the police. What do you think their responsibilities should be? What should they have the authority to do?

2. Read the title of this chapter. In the American legal system, a person accused of a crime is considered to be innocent until he or she is proven guilty in a court. In your country, does an accused person have to prove his or her innocence, or does the court have to prove the person's guilt?

3. Refer to the photo on pages 98–99. The woman represents justice. Why is she blindfolded? What do the scales in her left hand symbolize? What does the sword in her right hand symbolize?

Reading

🎧 **Read the passage carefully. Then complete the exercises that follow.**

Innocent until Proven Guilty: The Criminal Court System

1   The purpose of the American court system is to protect the rights of the people.
2   According to American law, if someone is accused of a crime, he or she is considered
3   innocent until the court proves that the person is guilty. In other words, it is the
4   responsibility of the court to prove that a person is guilty. It is not the responsibility
5   of the person to prove that he or she is innocent.

6   In order to arrest a person, the police have to be reasonably sure that a crime has
7   been committed. The police must give the suspect the reasons why they are arresting
8   him and tell him his rights under the law.[1] Then the police take the suspect to the
9   police station to "book" him. "Booking" means that the name of the person and the
10 charges against him are formally listed at the police station.

11 The next step is for the suspect to go before a judge. The judge decides whether
12 the suspect should be held in jail or released. If the suspect has no previous criminal
13 record and the judge feels that he will return to court rather than run away—for
14 example, because he owns a house and has a family—he can go free. Otherwise, the
15 suspect must put up bail.[2] At this time, too, the judge will appoint a court lawyer to
16 defend the suspect if he can't afford one.

17 The suspect returns to court a week or two later for a hearing, where a lawyer
18 from the district attorney's office presents a case against the suspect. This lawyer
19 is called the prosecutor. The attorney may present evidence as well as witnesses.
20 The judge at the hearing decides whether there is enough reason to hold a trial. If the
21 judge decides that there is sufficient evidence to call for a trial, he or she sets a date
22 for the suspect to appear in court to formally plead guilty or not guilty.

---

[1] The police must say, "You have the right to remain silent. Anything you say can and will be used against you in a court of law.
You have the right to speak to a lawyer and to have the lawyer present during questioning. If you so desire, and cannot afford one,
a lawyer will be appointed without any charge before any questioning. Do you understand these rights as I have explained them
to you?" These rights are called the Miranda rights.
[2] **Bail** is an amount of money that the accused person pays to the court to assure that he or she will return to the court on the trial
date. If the person comes back, the money is returned to him or her. If not, the court keeps the bail money.

23   At the trial, a jury of 12 people listens to the evidence from the defense attorney
24   and the prosecuting attorney and hears the testimony of the witnesses. Then the jury
25   goes into a private room to consider the evidence and decide whether the defendant
26   is guilty of the crime. If the jury decides that the defendant is innocent, he is acquitted
27   and goes free. However, if he is convicted, he remains in jail and the judge sets a
28   date for the defendant to appear in court again for sentencing. At this time, the judge
29   tells the convicted person what his punishment will be. The judge may sentence
30   him to prison, order him to pay a fine, or place him on probation.[3] If the person
31   is imprisoned, the judge tells him how long he will remain in jail.
32   The American justice system is very complex and sometimes operates slowly.
33   However, every step is designed to protect the rights of the people. These individual
34   rights are the basis, or foundation, of the American government.

---

[3]**Probation** means that the convicted person does not have to go to jail. Instead, the person must follow certain rules and is supervised by a parole officer.

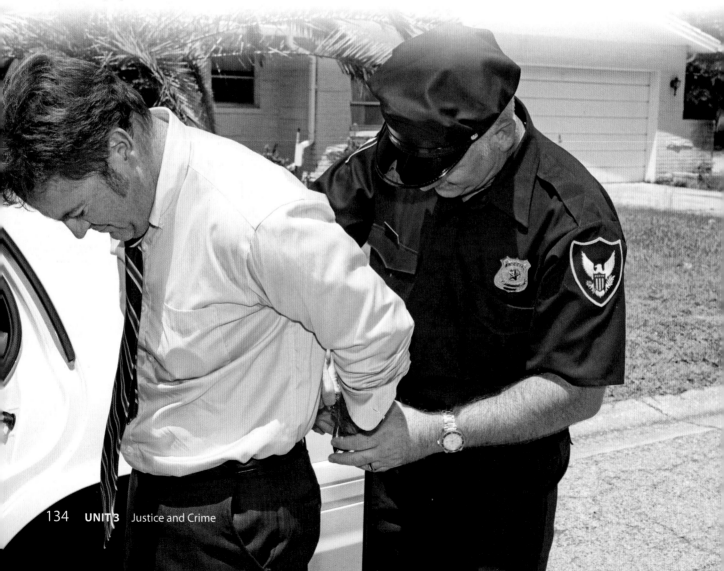

Fact Finding

Read the passage again. Then read the following statements. Check (√) whether each statement is True or False. If a statement is false, rewrite it so that it is true. Then go back to the passage and find the line that supports your answer.

1. _____ True _____ False   According to American law, the court must prove that a suspect is innocent.

   _____

2. _____ True _____ False   The police decide if a suspect stays in jail or can be released.

   _____

3. _____ True _____ False   The judge appoints a court lawyer for a suspect who cannot pay for one.

   _____

4. _____ True _____ False   An attorney can present evidence or witnesses at the hearing.

   _____

5. _____ True _____ False   There are 12 people on a jury.

   _____

6. _____ True _____ False   At a trial, the judge decides if the suspect is guilty or innocent.

   _____

7. _____ True _____ False   The jury gives the convicted person his punishment after the trial.

   _____

Reading Analysis

Read each question carefully. Circle the letter or the number of the correct answer, or write the answer in the space provided.

1. Read lines 2-3. **He or she is considered innocent** means
   a. the law assumes the suspect is innocent.
   b. the law must prove the suspect is innocent.

2. Read lines 3–5. What follows **in other words**?

    a. An example of the previous sentence

    b. A restatement of the previous sentence

    c. A new idea about the court system

3. Read lines 6–7. **Reasonably sure** means

    a. very certain.

    b. not certain.

    c. a little certain.

4. Read lines 7–8: **The police . . . tell him his rights under the law.**

    a. This sentence means

        1. the police take him to the police station.

        2. the police tell him the evidence against him.

        3. the police explain what he can legally do.

    b. What are these **rights** called?

    _____

    c. Where did you find this information?

    _____

    d. This information is called a

        1. direction.

        2. footnote.

        3. preface.

5. Read lines 8–10.

    a. In line 9, what does **booking** mean?

    _____

    b. Why does this word have quotation marks (**" "**) around it?

        1. It is a new word.

        2. Someone is saying this word in the reading.

        3. It is a special meaning of the word *book* that the police use.

6. Read lines 11–15.

    a. **Released** means

        1. allowed to leave.

        2. suspected of a crime.

        3. held by the judge.

    b. **He can go free** means

        1. the suspect is not guilty of any crime.

        2. the suspect does not have to go to trial because the judge has decided he is innocent.

        3. the suspect does not have to wait in jail or pay money until he goes to trial.

    c. **Otherwise** means

       1. if not.

       2. in addition.

       3. in contrast.

    d. Read the footnote describing **bail**. What is the purpose of having the suspect pay bail?

       1. To pay for the judge and the trial

       2. To ensure that the suspect will return to court

       3. To pay for a court lawyer to defend the suspect

7. Read lines 17–20. What is a **hearing**?

_____

_____

8. Read lines 17–22.

    a. The **prosecutor** is a lawyer who

       1. orders the judge to call for a trial.

       2. presents evidence to show the suspect probably committed a crime.

       3. sets a date for a hearing in court.

    b. What phrase is a synonym for **enough reason**?

    _____

9. Read lines 23–24. The **defense** attorney

    a. represents the suspect in court.

    b. testifies for the suspect.

    c. tries to prove that the suspect is guilty.

10. Read lines 26–30.

    a. **However** means

       1. also.

       2. next.

       3. but.

    b. When a person is **acquitted**, the person is

       1. cleared of a crime.

       2. given a new trial.

       3. defended by the jury.

    c. When a person is **convicted**,

       1. the judge is sure he is guilty.

       2. the jury has decided he is guilty.

       3. the defense attorney has won her case.

    d. What is **sentencing**?

       1. Subjects, verbs, and objects

       2. The date the defendant must appear in court

       3. The punishment that the judge gives the defendant

e. Read the footnote about **probation**. What is the purpose of probation?
   1. To make sure the convicted person behaves well
   2. To save the court some money

11. Read lines 32–34.
   a. **Complex** means
      1. lengthy.
      2. clear.
      3. complicated.
   b. What is a synonym for **basis**?

   _____

   c. How do you know?

12. What is the main idea of the passage?
   a. According to the American court system, a suspect must prove that he or she is innocent.
   b. The American court system is very complex and was designed to protect the rights of the people.
   c. According to the American court system, a judge decides if a suspect is innocent or guilty.

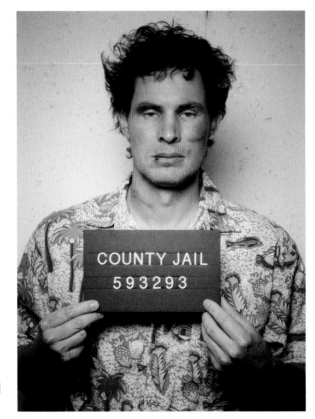

Suspect being photographed and booked

Vocabulary Skills

PART 1

Recognizing Word Forms

In English, there are several ways that adjectives change to nouns. Some adjectives become nouns by adding the suffix -ity, for example, *national (adj.)* becomes *nationality (n.)*. Some words change spelling, for example, *visible (adj.)*, *visibility (n.)*.

Complete each sentence with the correct word form on the left. All the nouns are singular.

responsible *(adj.)*
responsibility *(n.)*

1. In the United States, it is the _____ of the court to prove that a person is guilty. In other words, a suspect is not _____ for proving he is innocent.

formal *(adj.)*
formality *(n.)*

2. A suspect must appear in court to make a _____ innocent or guilty plea. This procedure is a _____ in U.S. law.

complex *(adj.)*
complexity *(n.)*

3. The American court system is very _____. An attorney can help a suspect understand the _____ of the law.

individual *(adj.)*
individuality *(n.)*

4. Americans value their _____ and believe that each person is important. It isn't surprising that every person has _____ rights under the law.

public *(adj.)*
publicity *(n.)*

5. Some important trials receive a lot of _____. People may read about them or watch them on TV. Also, the trial is _____ , so anyone may sit in the courtroom and observe the trial.

PART 2

Antonyms

Antonyms are words that have opposite meanings. For example, *public* and *private* are antonyms.

Match each word with its antonym. Write the letter of the correct answer and the word in the space provided.

____f. simple____	1. complex	a.	acquit
_____	2. convict	b.	guilty
_____	3. defend	c.	insufficient
_____	4. enough	d.	prosecute
_____	5. imprison	e.	release
_____	6. innocent	f.	~~simple~~
_____	7. sure	g.	uncertain

A police department meeting, Miami, Florida

Vocabulary in Context

Read the following sentences. Complete each sentence with the correct word from the box. Use each word only once.

appoint *(v.)*	consider *(v.)*	otherwise *(adv.)*	purpose *(n.)*
basis *(n.)*	establish *(v.)*	present *(v.)*	record *(n.)*
case *(n.)*	however *(adv.)*		

1. The Board of Health keeps an accurate _____ of all births and deaths in the city.

2. Holly worked very hard before she was able to _____ her own business, but eventually she was successful.

3. If it snows this week, we will go skiing this weekend. _____, we will stay in the city and see a movie.

4. The students always _____ a class representative for the student council at the beginning of the semester.

5. Every fall, television networks _____ new programs to their viewers.

6. When deciding on a college, you need to _____ several factors, including the cost of tuition, the courses offered, and the location of the college.

7. The ability to read and write well is the _____ of a good education.

8. I don't understand the _____ of this machine. What is it used for?

9. I prefer to eat only fresh vegetables. _____, when they are not available, I eat frozen or canned vegetables.

10. Have you read about the murder in the library last year? The police have been trying to

    solve that _____ for months, but so far they haven't been successful.

A lawyer questions a suspect.

Reading Skill

Creating a Flowchart

Flowcharts show certain kinds of information, such as the steps in a process. Creating a flowchart can help you organize and understand important information from a reading passage.

Read the sentences below. Write them in the correct order in the flowchart. When you are finished, go back to the reading and check your answers.

- The judge appoints a court lawyer to defend the suspect if he can't afford a lawyer.
- If the jury decides the defendant is innocent, he goes free.
- The convicted person goes to prison.
- If the jury decides the defendant is guilty, the judge sets a date for sentencing.
- The judge decides the sentence.
- The police take the suspect to the police station to book him.
- The convicted person pays a fine.
- The suspect goes before the judge, who decides if there should be a hearing.

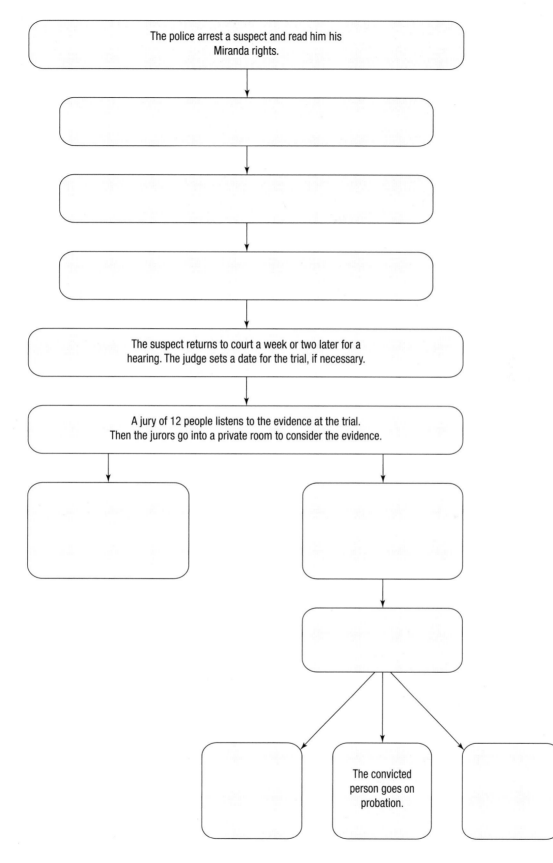

The police arrest a suspect and read him his Miranda rights.

The suspect returns to court a week or two later for a hearing. The judge sets a date for the trial, if necessary.

A jury of 12 people listens to the evidence at the trial. Then the jurors go into a private room to consider the evidence.

The convicted person goes on probation.

Information Recall

Read the passage again, and review the flowchart. Then answer the questions.

1. What must the police do if they arrest a suspect?

   _____

   _____

2. What happens to the suspect after the police book him or her?

   _____

   _____

3. If a person is acquitted, what happens? If a person is convicted, what happens to that person?

   _____

   _____

Writing a Summary

A summary is a short paragraph that provides the most important information from a reading. It usually does not include details, just the main ideas. When you write a summary, it is important to use your own words, and not copy directly from the reading.

Write a brief summary of the passage. The summary should not be more than four sentences. Use your own words. Be sure to indent the first line.

_____

_____

_____

_____

_____

Topics for Discussion and Writing

1. Work in small groups. The government has asked you to review the present procedure for arresting and booking a suspect. Review the steps involved in arresting and charging a person with a crime. Discuss what you would and would not change. Present your revised procedure to the class.

2. In the United States, trials are not held in secret. The public may sit in the courtroom and observe the proceedings. Visit a courtroom with two or three of your classmates. Observe what takes place. Report back to the class.

3. Write in your journal. Would you want to be part of a jury? Why or why not?

Critical Thinking

1. Refer to the flowchart in the Reading Skill exercise on page 143. It lists the American procedure for arresting and trying a person for a crime. Compare this system with the system in your country or another country that you know about. Use the following chart to compare the two systems, and list what you see as the advantages and disadvantages of each one.

	In the United States	In _____
procedure	Police arrest the suspect and read Miranda rights.	
advantage		
disadvantage		

	In the United States	In _____
procedure		
advantage		
disadvantage		

	In the United States	In _____
procedure		
advantage		
disadvantage		

2. Read about a criminal case in the news. Bring several newspaper and magazine articles on the case into class. In groups, form juries. Read through the evidence and decide whether the suspect is guilty or innocent. If your group decides the suspect is guilty, appoint a judge from your group to decide on a sentence.

3. An American jury goes into a private room to decide if a suspect is guilty or innocent. No one can come into the room except the jury. What do you think is the reason for this? Discuss this policy with a partner.

4. In the United States, most state trials are open to the public. In other words, anyone can sit in the courtroom during a trial. Do you think this is a good idea? Why or why not? Compare your ideas with your classmates' ideas.

5. In the United States, a person cannot be tried twice for the same crime. For example, if a person is accused of murder and goes to trial, but a jury acquits him, and later it is discovered that the person really did commit the murder, the person stays free. Discuss these questions with your classmates: Why do you think this is part of the American justice system? Why do you think this custom exists? Do you think this is fair and just? Explain your reasons.

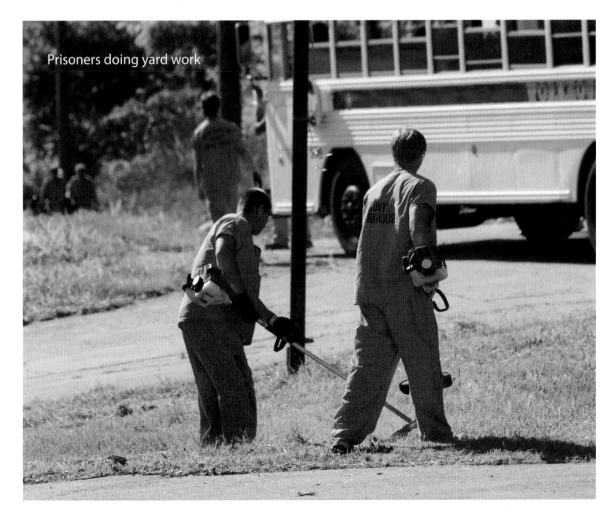
Prisoners doing yard work

Crossword Puzzle

Review the words in the box below. Then read the clues on the next page. Write the words in the correct spaces in the puzzle.

acquit	footnote	otherwise	rights
bail	foundation	probation	sentencing
book	hearing	reasonably	sufficient
complex	jury	released	sure
convict			

Crossword Puzzle Clues

ACROSS CLUES

3. The American legal system is _____. It is not simple!

8. A judge must be _____ certain that the evidence is strong before calling for a hearing.

9. A _____ is extra information at the bottom of a page to help a reader understand something.

10. I am _____ that is the man who robbed the bank. I am certain because I saw him clearly.

11. If jurors decide a defendant is innocent, they _____ the person.

13. The _____, or basis, of the American legal system is that a person is innocent until proven guilty.

14. At a _____, a judge listens to the evidence against a suspect and decides if a trial should take place.

16. The suspect had to pay $2,000 as a promise to show up in court. _____, he would have to stay in jail.

DOWN CLUES

1. If jurors decide a defendant is guilty, they _____ the person.

2. If a judge feels the evidence is not sufficient, the suspect is _____, or let go.

4. A _____ is made up of 12 people who hear a case at a trial.

5. When a guilty person is on _____, the person has to report to an officer on a regular basis.

6. The woman had to pay $1,000 in _____ so she wouldn't have to stay in jail until her trial.

7. There must be _____ evidence to hold a trial. If not, the case cannot go to court.

10. When a person is proven guilty, the _____ by the judge is not usually given on the same day.

12. The police _____ a suspect at the police station.

15. In the United States, everyone has the same legal _____ of a defense lawyer and trial by jury, even people who are not citizens.

Advances in Science

1. What are the most important advances in science today?

2. What do you think are the most important problems science and modern technology should try to solve?

3. What areas of science are most interesting to you—for example, biology, chemistry, astronomy, physics, geology? Why do you especially like these fields of science?

Zac Vawter stands on the Willis Tower, Chicago. Zac was the first person to climb wearing a prosthesis controlled with his mind.

A starfish regenerating an arm

A gecko shortly after dropping its tail to avoid a predator

Prereading

1. Look at the photos of the animals above. What can these animals do?

2. Can human beings do this, too?

3. Read the title of the article. What do you think this article is about?

4. Why do some people need a new organ? What kinds of organs do they sometimes need?

---

[1] An **organ** is a part of the body that has a specific function, for example, a heart, lung, kidney, or liver.

Reading

🎧 **Read the passage carefully. Then complete the exercises that follow.**

CD 1
TR 11

Saving Lives with New Organs

1   Starfish, salamanders, and lizards all have something in common: if a tail or a limb,
2   e.g., a leg, is severed, or cut off, these animals can regrow that part of their body. This
3   ability to regenerate, or regrow, a limb has fascinated scientists for centuries. They
4   wondered how people might one day be able to regenerate a body part, too. However,
5   no one had the technology or the know-how to do so until now.

6   Every year, hundreds of thousands of people who are sick or injured need organ
7   transplants such as hearts, kidneys, or lungs. Unfortunately, many die while they are
8   waiting for a new organ. These people could only hope for an organ or tissue from
9   a donor, usually from someone who has just died. Even if they are lucky enough to
10 find a donor, their immune system might still reject the transplant.

11 Today, scientists have developed a way to create some organs in a laboratory using
12 a patient's own cells. This way, the patient's body will not reject this new organ
13 because the new part came from the patient's own cells.

14 How do scientists create new organs? Which organ was one of the first to be
15 created? Dr. Anthony Atala works at the Wake Forest Institute for Regenerative
16 Medicine in Winston-Salem, North Carolina. He was able to create a "bioartificial"
17 organ—in particular, a bladder[2]—from a patient's own diseased bladder. Dr. Atala
18 developed something he calls the "bladder technique." This process involves taking
19 healthy cells from a person's diseased bladder and then growing many more of them
20 in a laboratory. Once the scientist has enough healthy cells, they are put into a mold
21 with a growth solution. This is a special chemical mixture that helps them to grow.
22 It takes about six to eight weeks to "grow" a healthy new bladder.

23 Kaitlyne McNamara was one of the first children to receive the bioartificial
24 bladder. She was born with a very serious disease and had dozens of operations as
25 a child. In spite of all the surgeries, her bladder was very weak. Dr. Atala took cells
26 from Kaitlyne's weak bladder to grow her new bladder. "Now that I've had the
27 transplant, my body actually does what I want it to do," Kaitlyne said. "Now I can
28 go have fun and not worry."

29 Scientists are working on many other human organs and tissues as well. For
30 example, they have successfully generated, or grown, a piece of liver. This is an
31 exciting achievement since people cannot live without a liver. In other laboratories,
32 scientists have created a human jawbone and a lung.

---

[2] A **bladder** is an organ in the body that holds urine from the kidneys until it passes from the body.

33   While these scientific breakthroughs are very promising, they are also limited.
34 Scientists cannot use cells for a new organ from a very diseased or damaged organ.
35 Consequently, many researchers are working on a way to use stem cells to grow
36 completely new organs. Stem cells are very simple cells in the body that can develop
37 into any kind of complex cells, such as skin cells or blood cells and even heart and
38 liver cells. In other words, stem cells can grow into all different kinds of cells. Some
39 stem cells come from a newborn baby's umbilical cord.[3] After a baby is born, its
40 umbilical cord detaches. Blood in the umbilical cord contains stem cells. These cells
41 are different from adult cells because adult cells will only grow into the type of tissue
42 they came from. Thus, a cell that comes from a bladder will only grow into a bladder.
43 In contrast, stem cells have the ability to become any kind of cell. Researchers have
44 made stem cells into heart, liver, and other organ cells. However, the use of stem cells
45 in medicine today is very controversial. Some people do not agree that using stem
46 cells for this purpose is a good idea.
47   Although medical research can be very controversial, helping people lead better
48 lives is something everyone can agree on.

---

[3] The **umbilical cord** connects the baby to the mother before the baby is born. It supplies nutrients and oxygen to the developing baby.

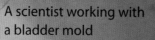
A scientist working with a bladder mold

Fact Finding

Read the passage again. Then read the following statements. Check (√) whether each statement is True or False. If a statement is false, rewrite it so that it is true. Then go back to the passage and find the line that supports your answer.

1. _____ True _____ False   Some patients die before they can receive an organ transplant.

   _____

2. _____ True _____ False   A patient's immune system always accepts the new organ.

   _____

3. _____ True _____ False   Patients' bodies will not accept organs that come from their own cells.

   _____

4. _____ True _____ False   Scientists can sometimes grow organs in a laboratory.

   _____

5. _____ True _____ False   Kaitlyne McNamara received an organ transplant from a donor.

   _____

6. _____ True _____ False   Scientists can use cells from any organ to make a new organ.

   _____

7. _____ True _____ False   Stem cells can grow to become any kind of cell.

   _____

8. _____ True _____ False   Everyone agrees that using stem cells is a good idea.

   _____

Reading Analysis

Read each question carefully. Circle the letter or the number of the correct answer, or write the answer in the space provided.

1. Read lines 1–5.
   a. To **have something in common** means
      1. like the same things.
      2. live in the same environment.
      3. share something that is the same.
   b. A **limb** is
      1. a tail.
      2. an arm or a leg.
      3. any part of the body.
   c. **E.g.** means
      1. for example.
      2. in addition.
      3. except for.
   d. **Severed** means
      1. regrown.
      2. cut off.
      3. injured.
   e. **Regenerate** means
      1. regrow.
      2. injure.
      3. reattach.
   f. Between the two words *regenerate* and *regrow* is **, or**. This means
      1. the two words are antonyms.
      2. the two words are synonyms.
      3. the two words are scientific.
   g. **Know-how** means
      1. training.
      2. education.
      3. skill and ability.

2. Read lines 6–10.
   a. An organ or tissue **transplant** means taking an organ or tissue
      1. from a dead person only and giving it to someone else.
      2. from a dead or living person and giving it to someone else.
      3. from a dead or living person and growing it in a laboratory.

b. A **donor**
    1. gives an organ or tissue.
    2. receives an organ or tissue.

3. Read lines 9–10.
    a. The purpose of the **immune system** is to
        1. kill any new organ or tissue in the body.
        2. protect the body from disease.
        3. help new organs or tissue grow well.
    b. If the immune system **rejects** an organ or tissue,
        1. the person will begin to feel better.
        2. it starts to regrow an organ or tissue.
        3. it does not accept the organ or tissue.

4. In line 12, a **patient** is
    a. an organ donor.
    b. a sick or injured person.
    c. a scientist.

5. Read lines 16–17.
    a. Why is **bioartificial** in quotation marks (" ")?
        1. Because it is a direct quote from Dr. Atala
        2. Because it is a word from another language
        3. Because it is a new word
    b. The term **bioartificial organ** means that the organ
        1. was created, but is not a healthy organ.
        2. was created, and is not a real organ.
        3. was created, but is still a real, living organ.
    c. What is a **bladder**?

_____

    d. Where did you find this definition?

_____

    e. This is called
        1. an index.
        2. a footnote.
        3. a preface.

6. Read lines 20–22.
    a. A **mold** is
        1. an empty form that gives shape to whatever is put into it.
        2. a dish for storing a number of objects.
        3. a flat surface for mixing things.

b. Why did the scientists put the bladder cells into a mold?
      1. So the chemical mixture has time to grow
      2. So the cells take on the shape of a bladder as they grow
      3. So the chemical mixture wouldn't spoil
   c. What is a **growth solution**?

   _____

7. Read lines 24–25. **In spite of** means
   a. thanks to.
   b. because of.
   c. regardless of.

8. Read lines 29–31.
   a. **Achievement** means
      1. failure.
      2. success.
      3. transplant.
   b. What is **this exciting achievement**?

   _____

9. Read lines 33–38.
   a. A scientific **breakthrough** is
      1. a problem in science.
      2. an advance in science.
      3. a question in science.
   b. If something is **promising**, it is
      1. encouraging.
      2. certain.
      3. clear.
   c. What are **stem cells**?

   _____

10. Read lines 38–40.
   a. How does **in other words** help you?
      1. It introduces additional information.
      2. It introduces a different idea.
      3. It introduces the same information in different words.
   b. What is an **umbilical cord**?

   _____

c. Where did you look for this information?

_____

d. This is called a _____.

11. Read lines 39–43.
    a. **Detaches** means
        1. separates.
        2. connects.
        3. falls.
    b. **Thus** means
        1. however.
        2. therefore.
        3. additionally.
    c. **In contrast** introduces
        1. an opposite idea.
        2. a similar idea.
        3. the same idea in different words.

12. Read lines 44–46. If an issue or idea is **controversial**,
    a. many people argue for and against the idea.
    b. a few people disagree with the idea.
    c. a few people agree with the idea.

13. What is the main idea of the passage?
    a. Some scientists have been able to grow new organs such as bladders, livers, and lungs.
    b. Scientists are making advances in organ regeneration using both adult cells and stem cells.
    c. Scientists have helped people lead better lives with controversial research.

Vocabulary Skills

PART 1

Recognizing Word Forms

In English, there are several ways that verbs change to nouns. Some verbs become nouns by adding the suffix *-tion* or *-ation*, for example, *inform (v.)*, *information (n.)*; *educate (v.)*, *education (n.)*.

Complete each sentence with the correct word form on the left. Write the correct form of the verbs in either the affirmative or the negative. The nouns may be singular or plural.

fascinate *(v.)*

fascination *(n.)*

1. A lizard's ability to regrow limbs _____ many people, including scientists. Because of this _____, scientists had the idea to regrow organs to help people.

create *(v.)*

creation *(n.)*

2. Scientists _____ bioartificial organs in laboratories. The _____ of new organs can help to save many people's lives.

operate *(v.)*

operation *(n.)*

3. As a child, Kaitlyne was very sick and had a lot of _____. Although many doctors _____ on her, she was still very ill.

generate *(v.)*

generation *(n.)*

4. Scientists are working on the _____ of many organs using patient's cells. Recently, they _____ a piece of a liver, a jawbone, and a lung.

reject *(v.)*

rejection *(n.)*

5. A patient's body _____ a new organ that comes from his or her own cells. However, _____ sometimes happens when a patient receives an organ from a donor.

PART 2

Recognizing Sentence Connectors

Sentence connectors, such as *consequently, in contrast, in other words, in spite of,* and *unfortunately,* connect ideas and help to make them clearer.

Complete each sentence with *consequently, in contrast, in other words, in spite of,* or *unfortunately*. Use each sentence connector only once.

1. _____ the small chance of getting a transplant, Katrin put her name on a waiting list.

2. Julio was on a waiting list for a heart transplant. _____, he has been waiting for three years.

3. Stella is an ideal person for a lung transplant. _____, she is healthy enough to live through the transplant operation and become well.

4. Thomas feels that stem cell research should continue. _____, his sister is against it.

5. A bladder is shaped like an empty bag. _____, a mold that is used to generate a bladder must be round and empty, too.

Vocabulary in Context

Read the following sentences. Complete each sentence with the correct word or phrase from the box. Use each word or phrase only once.

achievement *(n.)*	in spite of	rejected *(v.)*	thus *(adv.)*
breakthroughs *(n.)*	molds *(n.)*	severed *(v.)*	transplants *(n.)*
detached *(v.)*	patient *(n.)*		

1. Patricia enjoys making candy at home. She carefully pours melted chocolate into small,

round _____. Her candy is always delicious!

2. Because of so many medical _____, doctors can help more people than ever before.

3. The last day of class is next Friday. _____, we must finish all of our assignments by Thursday.

4. When the power cord _____ from my laptop, I was unable to finish writing an email.

5. Carlos was a _____ in the hospital for several weeks before he started to feel better.

6. Brian received a robotic arm after he _____ his limb in a car accident.

7. It was an incredible _____ when I graduated college last year.

8. In the past, kidney _____ were very unusual. Now they are quite common.

9. When the college _____ her application, Helen had to apply to a different university.

10. _____ the cold weather, the children played happily in the park.

Reading Skill

Look at the bar graph and answer the questions that follow.

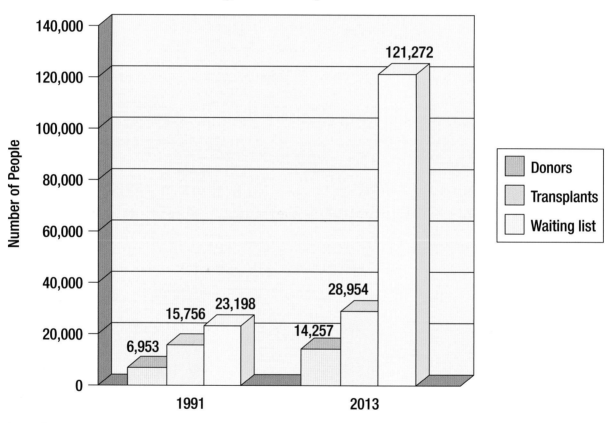

U.S. Organ Transplant Data

Source: http://www.organdonor.gov/about/data.html

1. How many more transplants were there in 2013 compared to 1991?

   a. The number has almost doubled.

   b. The number has almost tripled.

   c. The number has stayed the same.

2. How much has the number of people waiting for organ transplants increased from 1991 to 2013?
   a. The number has increased more than 500 percent.
   b. The number has doubled.
   c. The number has tripled.

3. In both 1991 and 2013, there were more organ transplants than there were organ donors. What do you think is a reason for this?
   a. Some people died during surgery, and the organ was used again.
   b. Some donors give more than one organ.
   c. Some people's bodies rejected the organ, and it was used for someone else.

Information Recall

Read the passage again. Then answer the questions.

1. What is a serious problem that people face when they need an organ transplant?

   _____

   _____

2. What have scientists developed to help save the lives of people who need new organs or tissues?

   _____

   _____

3. What are some advantages of using stem cells to generate organs and tissues?

   _____

   _____

Writing a Summary

A summary is a short paragraph that provides the most important information from a reading. It usually does not include details, just the main ideas. When you write a summary, it is important to use your own words, and not copy directly from the reading.

Write a brief summary of the passage. The summary should not be more than four sentences. Use your own words. Be sure to indent the first line.

Topics for Discussion and Writing

1. When a baby is born, its umbilical cord is detached because the baby doesn't need it anymore. Usually, it is thrown away, but now scientists can use stem cells from the umbilical cord to generate new organs and tissue. Do you agree or disagree with this use? Explain your reasons.

2. Most people have two healthy kidneys, but it is possible to live a healthy life with only one kidney. If a family member or friend needed a kidney, would you donate one of yours to that person? Why or why not? Explain your reasons.

3. Write in your journal. Imagine you have just had a baby who is born with a serious disease the way Kaitlyne McNamara was. Your doctor asks you for permission to use the baby's stem cells to try to grow a new organ to help the baby. Write about how you feel, the decision you make, and the reasons you make this decision.

Critical Thinking

1. Many sick people die while they are waiting for transplants. Why do you think this happens? Think about possible reasons for this. Discuss this with your classmates.

2. Do you want to be an organ donor after you die? Why or why not? Talk about this with a partner.

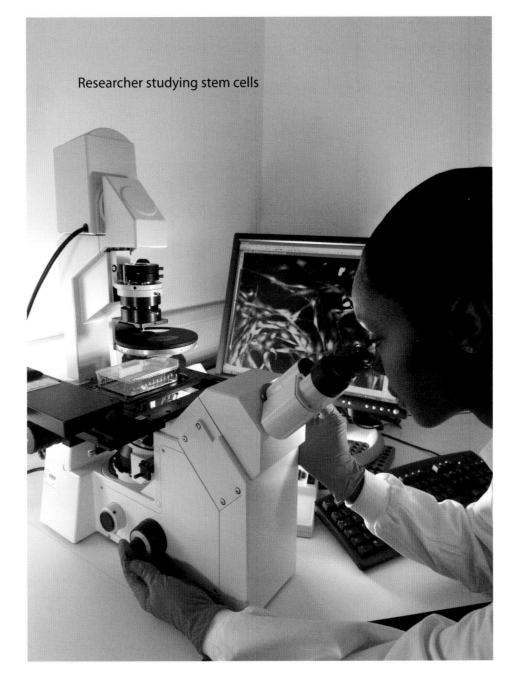
Researcher studying stem cells

Crossword Puzzle

Review the words in the box below. Then read the clues on the next page. Write the words in the correct spaces in the puzzle.

achievement	controversial	limited	reject
bioartificial	detach	mold	sever
bladder	donor	patient	tissue
breakthrough	immune	promising	transplant
consequently	limbs	regenerate	

Crossword Puzzle Clues

ACROSS CLUES

3. Some animals can _____ a whole leg!

4. Arms and legs are _____. A tail is not.

7. A _____ is an empty shape we can use to form things with.

12. A _____ organ is made of human cells but is grown in a laboratory.

13. People who receive an organ from another person often worry that their body will _____, or not accept it.

14. The ability to use cells to create a new organ is an amazing _____. This medical success will save many lives.

16. A major advance in science is called a _____. Advances can take place in any field!

17. Stem cell research is very _____. People sometimes become angry and argue about it.

18. Doctors can _____ many types of organs from one person to another, for example, a lung, heart, liver, or kidney.

19. A _____ is the organ that holds urine from the kidney until it passes from the body.

DOWN CLUES

1. If you _____, or cut off, a lizard's tail, the tail will regrow.

2. The future of medical research is very _____. Doctors are hopeful of making many improvements.

5. Our _____ system protects our bodies from infection and disease.

6. A _____ is a person, living or dead, who has agreed to provide organs or tissues to help others.

8. After birth, doctors _____ a baby's umbilical cord because the baby doesn't need it any longer.

9. A _____ is a person who is in a doctor's care.

10. Kaitlyne McNamara received a new bladder that was grown from her own cells. _____, her body accepted the bladder.

11. _____ is part of an organ, for example, a piece of liver or muscle.

15. Right now, research in regrowing organs is _____, but in the future, researchers will surely make a lot of progress in this area.

The Chelyabinsk Meteor speeding through the earth's atmosphere

Prereading

1. Read the title of this chapter. What are objects from space?

2. How often do these objects from space strike the earth? Do they do much damage?

3. What objects do you know about that have struck the earth?

4. Read the title of the article. What do you think this article is about?

Reading

🎧 **Read the passage carefully. Then complete the exercises that follow.**

Objects from Space: Hits and Misses

1 Although most people don't realize this, objects from space are constantly entering
2 the earth's atmosphere or passing nearby. Comets, asteroids, and meteors travel
3 through the solar system very close to the earth. Meteors are small fragments, or
4 pieces, of space debris, usually from a comet or asteroid. When they enter the earth's
5 atmosphere, they can appear as streaks of light in the sky. They are called falling stars.
6 Tons of space debris fly around the earth every day.

Recent Strikes

7 At about 9:20 a.m. local time on February 15, 2013, the people of Chelyabinsk,
8 Russia, were frightened to see a bright object moving quickly across the sky. In fact,
9 it was a meteor that was traveling at over 40,000 miles per hour! Witnesses reported
10 that the object was brighter than the sun. The Chelyabinsk meteor exploded in the
11 air. It created a large shock wave that damaged or destroyed over 7,200 buildings.
12 Unfortunately, more than 1,500 people across the region were injured. No one knew
13 the meteor was coming. However, the Chelyabinsk meteor was not the first time an
14 object entered the earth's atmosphere and caused damage.
15 In 1908, on the morning of June 30, in Siberia near the Tunguska River, a meteor
16 entered the earth's atmosphere and exploded. The meteor was traveling at 33,500
17 miles per hour. It affected 800 square miles of forest and destroyed 80 million trees.
18 Fortunately, it happened in a remote area of Siberia. Very few people live there. This
19 event is called the Tunguska Impact.

Ancient Strikes

20 Although the meteors in Chelyabinsk and Siberia entered the earth's atmosphere,
21 both exploded before they actually struck the earth. They were much smaller than
22 some other meteors that struck the earth in the past. The Chelyabinsk meteor was
23 55 feet wide and weighed 14,000 pounds. The Tunguska meteor was 120 feet wide
24 and weighed 220 million pounds!
25 A meteor struck the earth 50,000 years ago in what is now Arizona in the United
26 States. When it hit, this meteor was 150 feet wide, but it weighed 600 million pounds!
27 Scientists believe that all plants and animals within a few miles of the impact were
28 totally destroyed, and that animals living even several miles away were severely
29 burned. We can still see the crater, or large hole, that this meteor left in the ground.
30 The crater is three miles across.

Perhaps one of the most famous meteor impact sites is in Yucatán, Mexico. It is known as the Chicxulub Crater. This meteor struck the earth about 65 million years ago. Scientists think that this meteor impact caused the extinction of many species of plants and animals, including the dinosaurs. The meteor was probably between 106 and 186 miles across—possibly the largest meteor ever to strike the earth!

Near Misses

Damage from meteors and asteroids is unusual, but "near misses" occur quite frequently. A "near miss" is something that almost happened but didn't. In fact, scientists have identified over 10,000 near-Earth asteroids so far. One of the most recent took place on May 10, 2014. A small asteroid named 2014 JG55 passed just 60,000 miles from the earth. That's only one quarter the distance from the earth to the moon! This asteroid was only discovered the day it passed by. Like the meteor that struck the earth's atmosphere in Chelyabinsk, no one knew it was coming. Fortunately, asteroid 2014 JG55 was too small to cause much damage.

Another recent near miss surprised scientists. The asteroid 2004 BL86 passed three lunar distances[1] from the earth. 2004 BL86 was not dangerous to the earth because it did not pass too closely. However, scientists were amazed to see that this asteroid has its own moon!

Studying Hits and Near Misses

Scientists are constantly looking for asteroids, meteors, and comets that may pass close by the earth. By identifying these objects, they may be able to warn people and prevent deaths and injuries. Moreover, studying them helps scientists learn more about the universe we live in.

---

[1] One **lunar distance** is approximately 238,000 miles.

Meteor Crater, Arizona, U.S.A.

Fact Finding

Read the passage again. Then read the following statements. Check (√) whether each statement is True or False. If a statement is false, rewrite it so that it is true. Then go back to the passage and find the line that supports your answer.

1. _____ True _____ False   Very small amounts of space debris fly around the earth every day.

   _____

2. _____ True _____ False   The meteor that exploded near the Tunguska River injured millions of people.

   _____

3. _____ True _____ False   The meteor that created the Chicxulub Crater probably caused the extinction of dinosaurs.

   _____

4. _____ True _____ False   Near misses from meteors and asteroids are very common.

   _____

5. _____ True _____ False   Scientists did not know about the meteor in Chelyabinsk before it exploded near the earth.

   _____

6. _____ True _____ False   A few days ahead of time, scientists knew that asteroid 2014 JG55 was going to pass very close to the earth.

   _____

7. _____ True _____ False   The meteors in Chelyabinsk and Siberia exploded when they hit the earth.

   _____

Reading Analysis

Read each question carefully. Circle the letter or the number of the correct answer, or write the answer in the space provided.

1. Read lines 3–4. **Fragments** mean
   a. lights.
   b. asteroids.
   c. pieces.

2. Read lines 3–6. **They are called falling stars.** In this sentence, **they** means
   a. stars.
   b. meteors.
   c. comets.

3. Read the heading between lines 6 and 7.
   a. **Strikes** are
      1. hits.
      2. misses.
      3. debris.
   b. Where did the two recent strikes occur?

   _____

4. Read lines 9–10. The **witnesses** were
   a. the debris that flew close to the earth.
   b. the people who were injured when the meteor exploded.
   c. the people who saw the meteor in the sky.

5. Read lines 10–11.
   a. **Exploded** means
      1. broke apart suddenly.
      2. moved quickly.
      3. shone brightly.
   b. A **shock wave** is
      1. a bright light caused by a big explosion in the air.
      2. a big surprise to people when something from space explodes.
      3. a fast movement through the air caused by a big explosion above the ground.

6. Read line 12. A **region** is
   a. a building.
   b. an area.
   c. an object.

7. Read line 18. **Fortunately**, it happened in a **remote** area of Siberia.
   a. **Fortunately** describes something that is
      1. lucky.
      2. dangerous.
      3. expensive.
   b. A **remote** area is a place where
      1. many people live.
      2. not many people live.
      3. meteors hit.
   c. Complete this sentence with the correct choice.
      Fortunately, the meteor in Siberia did not hurt many people because
      1. the meteor was very small.
      2. not many people live there.

8. Read lines 31–34. The Chicxulub Crater is most famous because the meteor that caused it
   a. struck the earth in Mexico.
   b. probably caused the extinction of the dinosaurs.
   c. happened about 65 million years ago.

9. In line 38, **so far** means
   a. far away.
   b. in the future.
   c. until now.

10. Read lines 38–40. **One of the most recent took place on May 10, 2014. The most recent** refers to
    a. the near miss of asteroid 2014 JG55.
    b. the meteor that struck Chelyabinsk.
    c. the Tunguska impact in Siberia.

11. Read lines 41–42. **Like the meteor that struck the earth's atmosphere in Chelyabinsk, no one knew it was coming.** This sentence means
    a. no one knows when meteors will strike.
    b. no one knew that asteroid 2014 JG55 was coming.
    c. no one knew that asteroid 2014 JG55 was too small to cause damage.

12. Read lines 44–47.
    a. Scientists were amazed because the asteroid 2004 BL86
       1. did not pass too closely to the earth.
       2. was not dangerous to the earth.
       3. has its own moon.

b. **Lunar** is the adjective form for
   1. asteroid.
   2. Earth.
   3. moon.
c. What is a **lunar distance**?
   1. The approximate width, or diameter, of the earth
   2. The approximate width, or diameter, of the moon
   3. About 238,000 miles
d. Where did you find this information?
   1. In a dictionary
   2. At the bottom of the page
   3. In the reading passage
e. This information is called a _____.

13. Read lines 48–51.
   a. In line 49, **identifying** means
      1. seeing.
      2. naming.
      3. recognizing.
   b. In line 49, **warn** means
      1. surprise.
      2. caution.
      3. hurt.
   c. In line 50, **moreover** means
      1. however.
      2. also.
      3. recently.
   d. Why are scientists constantly looking for asteroids, meteors, and comets that may pass close by the earth?
      1. Scientists want to warn people and prevent deaths and injuries.
      2. Scientists want to learn more about the universe we live in.
      3. Both a and b

14. What is the main idea of the passage?
   a. Since ancient times, the earth has experienced both strikes and near misses of objects from space.
   b. Whenever objects have come near or enter the earth's atmosphere, they explode and create a bright light.
   c. Scientists have studied strikes and near misses of objects from space so they can identify them.

Vocabulary Skills

PART 1

Recognizing Word Forms

In English, some adjectives change to adverbs by adding the suffix *-ly*, for example, *careful* (*adj.*), *carefully*, (*adv.*).

Complete each sentence with the correct word form on the left.

constant (*adj.*)
constantly (*adv.*)

1. Objects in space are _____ passing near the earth's atmosphere. Scientists' _____ observation of space may prevent death and injuries.

fortunate (*adj.*)
fortunately (*adv.*)

2. It was _____ that the asteroid struck near a remote village in Siberia where few people live. _____, no one was hurt.

severe (*adj.*)
severely (*adv.*)

3. The Chelyabinsk meteor caused _____ damage to many buildings. Many people were _____ injured in the explosion.

quick (*adj.*)
quickly (*adv.*)

4. The meteor in Chelyabinsk moved _____ across the sky. The _____ movement and bright light surprised many people.

total (*adj.*)
totally (*adv.*)

5. A large meteor struck the earth about 50,000 years ago. Its _____ weight was 600 million pounds! This meteor _____ destroyed all plants and animals nearby.

PART 2

The Prefix *un-*

In English, the prefix *un-* means *not*. It can be added to many words, especially adjectives—for example, *uncommon* means *not common* when the prefix *un-* is added to *common*.

Read the following sentences. Complete each sentence with the correct word from the box. Use each word only once.

unaffected	undamaged	uninjured	unusual
unafraid	unfortunately	unsurprised	

1. The shock wave from the meteor impact broke windows, but the scientists were

   _____. They expected this type of damage.

2. Although the shock wave shattered many windows in the building, most of the people

   inside were _____. They were very lucky not to be hurt.

3. Because the Chelyabinsk meteor was small, plant and animal life in the area were

   completely _____ by the event. Nothing happened to them.

4. A major impact such as the event that caused the Chicxulub Crater is a very _____
   event. Scientists have identified only ten similar events over many millions of years.

5. The Chelyabinsk meteor exploded before it struck the earth. _____, the shock
   wave from the explosion caused many injuries and damage to many buildings.

6. Many people witnessed the Chelyabinsk meteor speed across the sky. However, some of the

   people were _____ because the meteor seemed too far away to hurt them.

7. Many buildings were affected by the meteor's explosion. Fortunately, the nearby hospital

   remained _____. The shock wave did not reach it.

Vocabulary in Context

Read the following sentences. Complete each sentence with the correct word from the box. Use each word only once.

damage *(n.)*	fortunately *(adv.)*	moreover *(adv.)*	remote *(adj.)*
event *(n.)*	frightened *(v.)*	region *(n.)*	witness *(n.)*
exploded *(v.)*	identify *(v.)*		

1. The loud thunder _____ the children.

2. The storm caused a lot of _____ to my neighborhood. Many windows were broken and several large trees fell down.

3. Carol was a _____ to an accident yesterday. She saw two buses collide near the school.

4. David and Emma's wedding was an important _____ in their lives.

5. My grandmother lives in a very _____ town. There are very few homes and people nearby.

6. I lost my keys, so I couldn't get into my apartment. _____, my neighbor has an extra key, and she opened the door for me.

7. Some people do not want to live in a _____ that has a lot of earthquakes.

8. This class has a lot of requirements. We must do our homework every night and take a test every week. _____, we have to write in our journals daily.

9. The car _____ after it hit a tree, but no one was hurt.

10. All my classmates have the same textbooks. I can easily _____ my books because I write my name on the cover of each one.

Reading Skill

Read the definitions of the words below. Then label the illustrations. Use each word only once.

asteroid	one of many rocky objects in space that usually orbit between Mars and Jupiter but that may come toward the earth
atmosphere	the air that surrounds the entire earth
comet	a space object made mostly of ice, dust, and rock. As it approaches the sun, it develops a long, bright tail.
meteor	an object from space that enters the earth's atmosphere
orbit	the curved path of a planet, moon, asteroid, or comet as it goes around another object in space
solar system	the sun, its eight planets, their moons, and all other space objects that orbit the sun

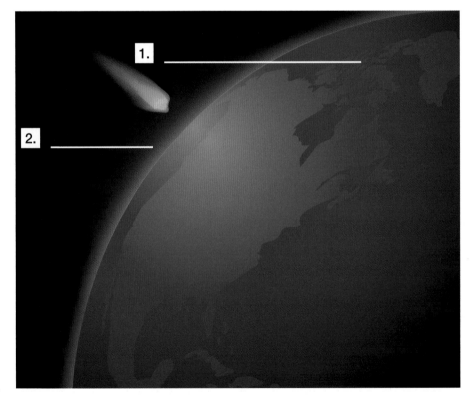

1. _____

2. _____

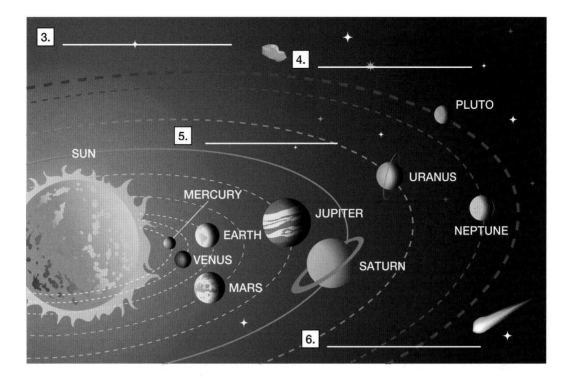

Information Recall

Read the passage again. Then answer the questions.

1. a. Where and when did the most recent meteor strike occur?

_____

_____

b. What was the result?

_____

_____

2. Why is the Chicxulub Crater the most famous meteor impact site?

_____

_____

3. Why do scientists study "near misses"?

_____

_____

Writing a Summary

A summary is a short paragraph that provides the most important information from a reading. It usually does not include details, just the main ideas. When you write a summary, it is important to use your own words, and not copy directly from the reading.

Write a brief summary of the passage. The summary should not be more than four sentences. Use your own words. Be sure to indent the first line.

_____

_____

_____

_____

_____

A collapsed building after the January 12, 2010 earthquake, Haiti

Topics for Discussion and Writing

1. Go online. Find information about another meteor strike that happened in the past. When and where did it occur? Did it cause any damage? Present your information to your class.

2. Imagine that a large meteor is heading for the earth. Scientists are sure this large meteor will strike the earth in the region where you live and cause tremendous damage and deaths. They know it will strike in three months. Form a committee of several classmates. Create a plan to assist the people in your region. Consider these questions: Where can they go? When should they leave? What should they take with them?

3. Write in your journal. Imagine that you were a witness to the Chelyabinsk meteor. What did it look and sound like? Describe your feelings on that day.

Critical Thinking

1. A meteor strike is a kind of natural disaster, such as an earthquake or a tsunami. Do you think a meteor strike is the most dangerous type of natural disaster? Why? If not, what do you think is the most dangerous natural disaster? Discuss your ideas with your classmates.

2. Discuss this question with a partner: Do you think it's important for scientists to know about "near misses"? Why or why not?

Phuket, Thailand, after the 2004 Indian Ocean Tsunami

Crossword Puzzle

Review the words in the box below. Then read the clues on the next page. Write the words in the correct spaces in the puzzle.

asteroid	fortunately	orbit	strike
atmosphere	fragments	region	universe
comet	identify	remote	warn
explode	moreover	severely	witnesses

Crossword Puzzle Clues

ACROSS CLUES

5. When a meteor hits the earth, everything nearby is _____ burned or completely destroyed.

6. Several planets _____ our sun. The earth has the third closest path from the sun.

7. Our solar system is only a small area in the _____.

8. Scientists may be able to _____ people that an object is approaching the earth, but they cannot stop it from coming.

11. When meteors speed through the earth's atmosphere, they often _____ in the air before they hit the ground.

13. Many people wonder if a large meteor will _____ the earth again!

14. The Tunguska event took place in a _____ area of the world, so people at the time were very lucky.

15. Meteors are usually small pieces, or _____, of larger space objects such as asteroids or comets.

DOWN CLUES

1. _____ for people on Earth, very large meteors do not hit the earth often.

2. A(n) _____ is a small rocky object in space that orbits the sun.

3. The object that hit the earth 65 million years ago caused tremendous damage to the ground. _____, it caused the extinction of many plants and animals.

4. The earth's _____ protects it from many of the objects that come toward it since most of the objects burn up passing through it.

8. There were many _____ to the Chelyabinsk event, but almost none for the Tunguska event in 1908.

9. When scientists _____ an object in space, they observe its path to see if it will come near the earth.

10. A meteor could possibly hit any _____ of the earth, even a very populated area!

12. A(n) _____ is an object made of ice, dust, and rock. It creates a tail as it gets near the sun.

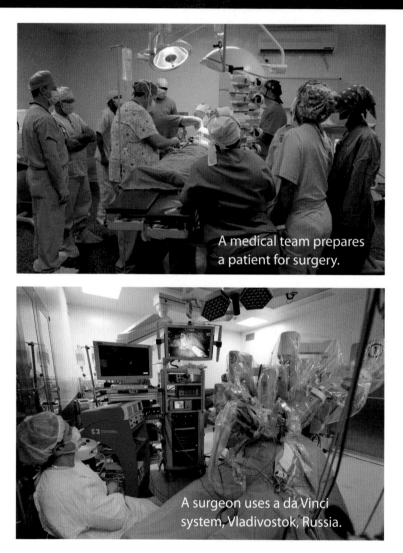

A medical team prepares a patient for surgery.

A surgeon uses a da Vinci system, Vladivostok, Russia.

Prereading

1. What is surgery? Why is surgery performed? Where is surgery performed?

2. Examine both photos and look at the title of the chapter. How many people are in the operating room in the first photo? How many are in the second photo? Who are these people?

3. Which photo has fewer people? Why are there fewer people?

4. Look at the two photos again. Which kind of surgery do you think is better? Why?

Reading

🎧 **Read the passage carefully. Then complete the exercises that follow.**

CD 1
TR 13

Medicine Today: Improving Surgery with Robotics

1   In most operating rooms today, there are two or three surgeons, an anesthesiologist,[1]
2   several nurses, and the patient. All of these people are needed for even a simple
3   surgery. This situation, however, has begun to change. Surgical robots are beginning
4   to replace several surgeons during one operation. In a few hospitals today, an
5   operation requires only one surgeon, a computer, and a surgical robot. Looking even
6   further into the future, the surgeon may not need to be there at all!
7   Robotic surgery has many advantages. First of all, it can be less traumatic for the patient.
8   For example, during traditional heart surgery, the surgeon must open the patient's chest
9   in order to perform the operation. Often, the opening, or incision, is about one foot long.
10 However, with modern robotic surgery, called the da Vinci system, it's possible to make
11 only three or four small incisions—about an inch each—instead. Because the incisions are
12 so much smaller, the patients experience much less pain and bleeding. As a result, they can
13 recover much faster. Furthermore, robotic surgery can be performed more quickly than
14 traditional surgery, which means the surgeons are not so exhausted when they're finished.
15 During robotic surgery, the doctor controls the robotic "arms" using a computer.
16 Currently, the doctor must be in the operating room with the patient for the robotic
17 systems to react instantly to the doctor's hand movements. With further developments in
18 this technology, the doctor will be able to control the robot from another room. Eventually,
19 the doctor may not even have to be in the same hospital as the patient. This would allow
20 surgeons to perform operations on patients miles away—even hundreds of miles!
21 Michael Troy strongly believes that the da Vinci robotic surgery system saved his
22 life. He was a 22-year-old college student when he learned that he had kidney cancer.
23 The news was devastating. "I thought this was the end for me," Michael said. "Many
24 doctors did not want to perform surgery on me because my cancer was so severe. They
25 would have to make a huge incision in my back in order to remove my kidney." Then
26 one of Michael's doctors suggested that Michael might have one other option. He sent
27 Michael to see Dr. Fuentes at University Hospital in Columbia, Missouri. Dr. Fuentes
28 said to Michael, "I think I can save your kidney." At first, Michael did not believe the
29 doctor. "Of course I was skeptical," Michael says. Dr. Fuentes explained that in order
30 to remove the cancer and save Michael's kidney, he would need four hands to get into
31 the small area. However, with a da Vinci robot under his control, Dr. Fuentes could
32 effectively perform the surgery making only small incisions to Michael's body.

---

[1] An **anesthesiologist** is a doctor who gives a drug to a patient to make the person unconscious and unable to feel pain.

33 Dr. Fuentes showed Michael a video of the da Vinci system. "After I watched the
34 video, I knew that this was the best—maybe even the only—possible treatment for
35 me." A week later, Michael had the surgery. As promised, Dr. Fuentes saved a large
36 part of Michael's kidney and removed the cancer. "This was all due to the da Vinci
37 system," adds Michael. Today, Michael is a healthy college graduate. "I'm so grateful
38 to Dr. Fuentes for saving my life and my kidney," says Michael. "I would recommend
39 the da Vinci system, especially because my tumor was so large. I didn't want to lose
40 a kidney at such a young age."

41 Robotic surgery is still developing. However, doctors believe there may be even
42 more amazing technology in the operating rooms of the future: robot surgeons. At
43 Duke University in North Carolina in the United States, doctors and scientists are
44 working to develop a robot that can perform surgery by itself. Dr. Steve Smith of
45 Duke University thinks that the technology could reduce the cost and time necessary
46 to complete some surgical procedures. "We keep giving the robot more and more
47 complex tasks," said Dr. Smith. "So far the robot has been able to accomplish these
48 tasks automatically." Many doctors, including Dr. Smith, agree that it will take about
49 ten years before robot surgeons become a reality. Like most medical technology, in the
50 beginning it will likely be more expensive than using a human surgeon. Eventually,
51 doctors hope that the life-saving technology will become widely available and more
52 affordable for all.

The da Vinci surgical robot

Fact Finding

Read the passage again. Then read the following statements. Check (√) whether each statement is True or False. If a statement is false, rewrite it so that it is true. Then go back to the passage and find the line that supports your answer.

1. _____ True _____ False   During traditional surgery, there may be seven or more people in the operating room.

_____

2. _____ True _____ False   Traditional surgery is faster than robotic surgery.

_____

3. _____ True _____ False   Patients recover much faster after traditional surgery than they do after robotic surgery.

_____

4. _____ True _____ False   During robotic surgery, doctors use their arms to control the robot.

_____

5. _____ True _____ False   It may be possible in the future for doctors to operate on patients who are far away.

_____

6. _____ True _____ False   Dr. Fuentes believes that robotic surgery saved his life.

_____

7. _____ True _____ False   In the future, robot surgeons may perform operations without doctors.

_____

Reading Analysis

Read each question carefully. Circle the letter or the number of the correct answer, or write the answer in the space provided.

1. Read lines 1–6.

  a. What does an **anesthesiologist** do?

  _____

  b. Where did you find this information?
     1. In the reading passage
     2. In a footnote
     3. In an index

  c. What word is a synonym of **requires**?

  _____

  d. Looking into the future, what may change in an operating room?
     1. The number of surgeons in an operating room
     2. The number of patients in an operating room
     3. The number of days that a patient must stay in the hospital

  e. This might change because
     1. people are healthier today.
     2. one surgical robot may replace several surgeons.
     3. surgery today is easier and faster.

2. Read lines 7–11.

  a. **Traumatic** means
     1. shocking and painful.
     2. frightening and worrying.
     3. long and expensive.

  b. An **incision** is
     1. a type of heart surgery.
     2. a long, difficult operation.
     3. an opening cut into the body.

  c. How do you know?

  _____

  d. What information is between the two dashes (—)?
     1. A definition of incisions
     2. Details about the incisions
     3. An explanation of the incisions

3. Read lines 12–14.
   a. **As a result** means
      1. consequently.
      2. however.
      3. additionally.
   b. When you **recover**, you
      1. have small incisions.
      2. experience pain and bleeding.
      3. become healthy again.
   c. **Exhausted** means
      1. very worried.
      2. very tired.
      3. very unhappy.
   d. The surgeons are not so exhausted when they're finished because
      1. robotic surgery requires fewer doctors.
      2. robotic surgery is easier than traditional surgery.
      3. robotic surgery takes less time than traditional surgery.

4. Read lines 16–19.
   a. **React** means
      1. control.
      2. respond.
      3. copy.
   b. **Eventually** means
      1. after a while.
      2. fortunately.
      3. surprisingly.

5. Read lines 21–23.
   a. What is the **da Vinci system**?
      1. A robotic surgery system
      2. A kind of traditional surgery
      3. An illness or disease
   b. Who is Michael Troy?
      1. A doctor
      2. A robot surgeon
      3. A patient
   c. **The news was devastating. "I thought this was the end for me."** The second sentence means
      1. Michael thought he was going to drop out of college.
      2. Michael thought he was going to die.
      3. Michael thought he was going to become very sick.

d. **Devastating** means
   1. very upsetting.
   2. very confusing.
   3. very important.

6. Read lines 25–32.

   a. An **option** is
      1. an incision.
      2. a choice.
      3. an operation.

   b. **"Of course I was skeptical"** means
      1. Michael did not want the surgery.
      2. Michael had kidney cancer.
      3. Michael did not believe his doctor.

   c. **Effectively** means
      1. successfully.
      2. carefully.
      3. dangerously.

7. Read lines 33–37.

   a. How did Michael feel after watching the video of the da Vinci system?
      1. He was still very worried about the surgery.
      2. He felt this type of surgery would be perfect for him.
      3. He still did not want his kidney to be removed.

   b. **Treatment** means
      1. medical care.
      2. a special video.
      3. kidney removal.

   c. The information between the two dashes (—)
      1. emphasizes the importance of the treatment.
      2. gives more details about the treatment.
      3. shows Michael's worries about the treatment.

   d. This was all **due to** the da Vinci system. **Due to** means
      1. in addition to.
      2. in spite of.
      3. as a result of.

8. Read lines 41–44.

   a. **Amazing** means
      1. complex.
      2. wonderful.
      3. technological.

b. **Doctors and scientists are working to develop a robot that can perform surgery by itself.** This means that the robot will
   1. perform the surgery alone.
   2. help doctors perform the surgery.
   3. perform surgery on doctors and scientists.

9. Read lines 46–52.
   a. A **task** is
      1. a request.
      2. surgery.
      3. a job.
   b. **So far** means
      1. up to now.
      2. at a distance.
      3. in the future.
   c. **Automatically** means
      1. quickly.
      2. independently.
      3. successfully.
   d. When something becomes a **reality**, it becomes
      1. difficult.
      2. expensive.
      3. possible.
   e. **Many doctors, including Dr. Smith, agree that it will take about ten years before robot surgeons become a reality.** This sentence means
      1. robot surgeons are used today.
      2. Dr. Smith developed robot surgeons about ten years ago.
      3. robot surgeons will be used in about ten years.
   f. Like most medical technology, in the beginning it will likely be **more expensive** than using a human surgeon. What is an antonym for **more expensive**?
      1. More affordable
      2. More popular
      3. More effective

10. What is the main idea of the reading?
    a. Traditional surgery takes longer and can be more difficult than robotic surgery.
    b. In the future, robot surgeons might perform operations by themselves.
    c. Robotic surgery is becoming more helpful and effective for patients and doctors.

Vocabulary Skills

PART 1

Recognizing Word Forms

In English, there are several ways that verbs change to nouns. Some verbs become nouns by adding the suffix -ment, for example, appoint (v.), appointment (n.).

Complete each sentence with the correct word form on the left. Use the correct tense of the verb in either the affirmative or the negative form. The nouns may be singular or plural.

require *(v.)*

requirement *(n.)*

1. Robotic surgery _____ fewer doctors than traditional surgery does. Because of this new _____, hospitals can save a lot of money.

move *(v.)*

movement *(n.)*

2. A surgeon controls the _____ of the surgical robot with a computer. If a surgeon doesn't control it, the da Vinci system _____.

improve *(v.)*

improvement *(n.)*

3. Michael Troy's health quickly _____ after his surgery. He was able to return to college because of the fast _____ in his health.

develop *(v.)*

development *(n.)*

4. Scientists are working to _____ a robotic surgeon that can perform operations alone. This _____ will help save the lives of many people.

treat *(v.)*

treatment *(n.)*

5. Some medical _____ involve surgery. This is because doctors _____ all illnesses with only medicine.

PART 2

Using a Dictionary

In English, words may have more than one meaning, depending on the context. For example, *perform* may refer to completing a task (*The doctor performed the surgery in two hours.*). It may also mean act or behave (*He performed very calmly during the emergency.*). It can mean to act or present a performance (*The dancers performed the ballet very well.*).

1. Read the following sentences. Use the context to help you understand the words in bold. Then read the dictionary entry for **recover** and circle the appropriate definition.

    Because the incisions are so much smaller, the patients experience much less pain and bleeding. As a result, they can **recover** much faster.

    > **recover** /rɪˈkʌvər/ *v.* **1** [I] to regain one's health: *He recovered from his illness and is well again.* **2** [T] to get s.t. back, to get control again: *Workers recovered a sunken boat from the lake.* **3** [T] to make up for losses: *The race car driver recovered the time he lost at the start of the race and won.* **4** [T] to put a new cover (new material) on s.t.: *to recover a sofa -adj.* **recoverable**. *See:* reupholster.

2. Circle the letter of the sentence that has the appropriate meaning of **recover**.
    a. As a result, he can put a new cover on himself much faster.
    b. As a result, he can make up for his losses much faster.
    c. As a result, he can regain his health much faster.
    d. As a result, he can get control back much faster.

3. **Recover** means
    a. get better.
    b. put a cover on.
    c. regain.
    d. retrieve.

4. Read the following sentence. Use the context to help you understand the word in bold. Then read the dictionary entry for **react** and circle the appropriate definition.

Currently, the doctor must be in the operating room with the patient for the robotic systems to **react** instantly to the doctor's hand movements.

> **react** /ri'ækt/ *v.* [I] **1** to speak or move when s.t. happens: *When he heard the good news, he reacted with a smile.* **2** to act in a different way because of s.o. or s.t.: *The teacher reacted to the student's bad grades by giving him more homework.* **3** (in chemistry) to change because of contact with another chemical: *Oxygen and iron react together to form rust.*

5. Circle the letter of the sentence that has the appropriate meaning of **react**.

a. Currently, the doctor must be in the operating room with the patient for the robotic systems to act in a different way instantly to the doctor's hand movements.

b. Currently, the doctor must be in the operating room with the patient for the robotic systems to change instantly to the doctor's hand movements because of contact with another chemical.

c. Currently, the doctor must be in the operating room with the patient for the robotic systems to move instantly with the doctor's hand movements.

6. React means

a. behave.

b. counter.

c. respond.

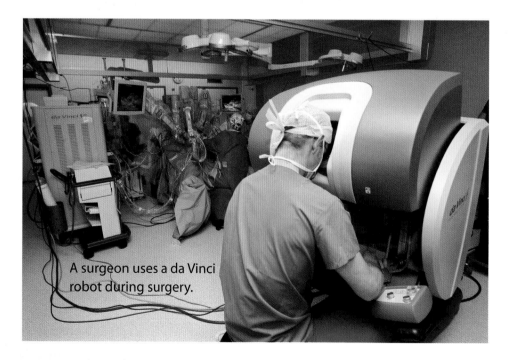
A surgeon uses a da Vinci robot during surgery.

Vocabulary in Context

Read the following sentences. Complete each sentence with the correct word from the box. Use each word only once.

affordable *(adj.)*	option *(n.)*	require *(v.)*	surgeon *(n.)*
exhausted *(adj.)*	patient *(n.)*	skeptical *(adj.)*	surgery *(n.)*
incision *(n.)*	recover *(v.)*		

1. Gloria is _____. She ran ten miles this morning and then worked all day.

2. Dr. Mallory is the _____ who will perform the operation this afternoon.

3. Thank you for offering to help me, but I do not _____ any assistance.

4. The nurse took care of the _____ and then recorded his condition in a book.

5. Anna is very _____ of John's ability to drive a car. He has had three accidents already this year!

6. That car costs $40,000. It's too expensive for me. I need a more _____ one.

7. The surgeon made a two-inch _____ and then continued with the operation.

8. Cynthia has never had _____. In fact, she has never been in a hospital.

9. I'm sorry to hear that you're ill. I hope you _____ very quickly.

10. When you take this exam, you have the _____ of writing it on paper or on a computer.

Reading Skill

Understanding a Line Graph

Line graphs often contain important information. It's important to understand them. Line graphs compare numbers or amounts, and they give you information about the reading.

Read the line graph below. Then answer the questions.

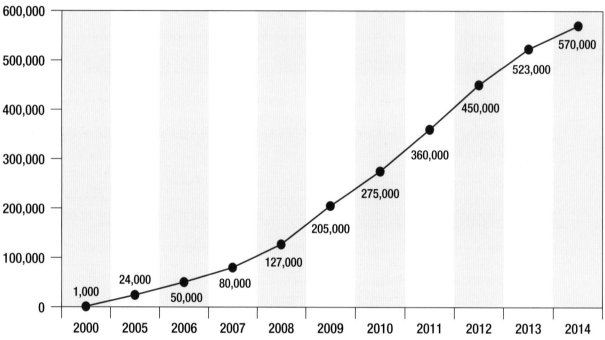

Number of da Vinci Procedures Worldwide

Sources: https://qualityoflife.org/surgery/davinci/robotic-surgery-leader/; Intuitive Surgical / The Wall Street Journal

1. During what time period did the number of da Vinci procedures increase the most?
   a. Between 2000 and 2005
   b. Between 2009 and 2010
   c. Between 2011 and 2012

2. During what time period did the number of da Vinci procedures increase the least?
   a. Between 2000 and 2005
   b. Between 2006 and 2007
   c. Between 2013 and 2014

3. Which statement most accurately summarizes the statistics in the graph?
   a. Since 2000, the number of da Vinci procedures has gradually increased.
   b. Since 2000, the number of da Vinci procedures has greatly increased.
   c. Since 2000, the number of da Vinci procedures has increased equally between each time period.

Information Recall

Read the passage again, and review the line graph. Then answer the questions.

1. What are the main differences between traditional surgery and robotic surgery?

   _____

   _____

   _____

   _____

2. What is the future of robotic surgery?

   _____

   _____

   _____

   _____

3. Which kind of surgery helped Michael Troy? Why?

   _____

   _____

   _____

   _____

Writing a Summary

A summary is a short paragraph that provides the most important information from a reading. It usually does not include details, just the main ideas. When you write a summary, it is important to use your own words, and not copy directly from the reading.

Write a brief summary of the passage. The summary should not be more than four sentences. Use your own words. Be sure to indent the first line.

_____

_____

_____

_____

_____

Topics for Discussion and Writing

1. Robotic surgery is new medical technology that can help a lot of people. What is another type of medical technology that helps people? Write about it.

2. Robotic surgery is used in some operations. What other uses might there be for robotics in the field of medicine?

3. Choose a medical procedure that interests you. Prepare a report on the procedure. Describe what it is used for and how it is performed.

4. Write in your journal. Describe an experience you, or someone you know, had with a surgical procedure in a hospital. What was the procedure? How was it performed? How quickly did you, or the person you are writing about, recover?

Critical Thinking

1. You are going to interview Michael Troy about his robotic surgery. Make a list of questions for him. Then exchange your questions with one of your classmates. Pretend that you are Michael Troy and write answers to your classmate's questions.

2. Traditional surgeries require a lot of people in the operating room. Why do you think this is so? Discuss your ideas with a partner.

3. Robotic surgery would allow surgeons to perform operations on patients miles away. Do you think a patient would want a surgeon who is so far away? Why or why not? Talk about this with your classmates.

4. Michael had surgery for his kidney cancer. What other kinds of operations will be possible with robotic surgery? Work with a partner and make a list. Then compare your list with your classmates' lists.

5. How can modern technology help a surgeon perform an operation that is less dangerous for the patient? What do you think? Discuss your ideas with your classmates.

Crossword Puzzle

Review the words in the box below. Then read the clues on the next page. Write the words in the correct spaces in the puzzle.

affordable	effectively	react	task
amazing	exhausted	reality	traditional
anesthesiologist	incision	recover	traumatic
automatically	option	require	treatment
devastating	perform	skeptical	

Crossword Puzzle Clues

ACROSS CLUES

1. One day, robotic surgery may make long-distance operations a _____ instead of a dream.

4. When the surgeon is finished operating, her last _____ is to close up the cut she has made.

11. The news that a person has cancer can be _____, especially if it is a serious form of cancer.

12. A(n) _____ is a doctor who gives a patient drugs to make the patient unconscious and unable to feel pain.

17. If surgery is minor, or simple, then patients usually _____ very quickly.

18. As technology advances, it often becomes less expensive and more _____.

19. Robotic surgery is very different from _____ surgery. For instance, fewer people are needed in the operating room.

DOWN CLUES

2. What kind of _____ did the doctor recommend for your disease? Surgery or drugs, or both?

3. A(n) _____ is a cut into the body that the surgeon makes during an operation.

5. Robotic surgery is a(n) _____ new technology. Many people are surprised at how useful it is.

6. The surgeon was _____ after doing an operation that lasted ten hours.

7. An operation can be very _____ to a person's body. It involves cutting the person open, for example.

8. Sometimes drugs can _____ treat a disease. Other times, surgery is necessary.

9. How do most people _____ when a doctor tells them they need surgery? Are they calm or frightened?

10. In robotic surgery, the robot _____ responds to the surgeon's commands.

13. When treating cancer, surgery is one _____. Using drugs instead is another choice.

14. Doctors _____ assistants during surgery. They cannot do surgery alone.

15. Michael was _____ when the doctor offered him robotic surgery. He didn't believe it could be effective.

16. Doctors _____ surgery. Nurses assist the surgeon.

INDEX OF KEY WORDS AND PHRASES

Words with **AWL** beside them are on the Academic Word List (AWL), Coxhead (2000). The AWL is a list of the 570 highest-frequency academic word families that regularly appear in academic texts. The list was compiled by researcher Avril Coxhead from a corpus of 3.5 million words.

SKILLS INDEX

GRAMMAR AND USAGE
Word forms
- Adjectives that become adverbs by adding -*ly*, 175
- Adjectives that become nouns by adding -*ity*, 139
- Adjectives that become nouns by adding -*ness*, 88–89
- Adjectives that become nouns by changing final -*t* to -*ce*, 58–59
- Prefix *in*- added to adjectives, 124
- Prefix *re*- added to verbs, 107
- Prefix *un*- added to adjectives, 176
- Verb and noun forms of some words that are the same, 10–11, 39–40
- Verbs that become nouns by adding -*ence* or -*ance*, 123
- Verbs that become nouns by adding -*ing*, 25
- Verbs that become nouns by adding -*ment*, 74–75, 106, 192
- Verbs that become nouns by adding -*tion* or -*ation*, 159–160

LISTENING/SPEAKING
Discussion, 19, 65, 68, 82, 132, 147, 199
- Topics, 15, 29, 45–46, 64, 78, 93, 112, 127, 145, 164, 181, 198

READING
Comprehension
- Antonyms, 25–26, 140
- Bar graph, 162–163
- Charts, 4, 18, 32, 46–47, 53, 76–77
- Critical thinking, 15, 29, 46–47, 65, 79, 94–95, 113, 128–129, 145–147, 165, 181, 199
- Crossword puzzle clues, 17, 31, 49, 67, 81, 97, 115, 131, 149, 167, 183, 201
- Crossword puzzles, 16, 30, 48, 66, 80, 96, 114, 130, 148, 166, 182, 200
- Dictionary, 40–41, 59–60, 193–194
- Fact finding, 7, 21, 35, 55, 70–71, 85, 103, 119, 135, 155, 171, 187
- Flowcharts, 27, 90–91, 142–143
- Graphics or illustrations, 45, 178–179
- Group activities, 94–95, 116–117, 128–129
- Information recall, 14, 28, 44, 63–64, 77–78, 92–93, 111, 126, 144, 163, 179, 197
- Line graphs, 108–110, 196
- Outlining, 61–63, 125–126
- Prereading, 4–5, 18–19, 32–33, 52–53, 68, 82–83, 100, 116–117, 132, 152, 168, 184
- Reading analysis, 7–10, 22–24, 36–39, 56–58, 71–74, 86–88, 103–106, 119–123, 135–138, 156–159, 172–174, 188–191
- Sentence connectors, 89, 160–161
- Synonyms, 11, 75
- Venn diagram, 12–13, 43
- Vocabulary in context, 12, 26, 42, 60–61, 76, 90, 108, 124–125, 141, 161, 177, 195

TOPICS

VISUAL LITERACY

WRITING

NOTES